HANDCRAFTED CSS

 More Bulletproof Web Design

DAN CEDERHOLM

with **Ethan Marcotte**

New
Riders

VOICES THAT MATTER™

Handcrafted CSS: More Bulletproof Web Design
Dan Cederholm with Ethan Marcotte

New Riders
1249 Eighth Street
Berkeley, CA 94710
510/524-2178
510/524-2221 (fax)
Find us on the Web at: www.newriders.com

New Riders is an imprint of Peachpit, a division of Pearson Education.

To report errors, please send a note to: errata@peachpit.com

Editor: Rebecca Gulick
Production Editor: Hilal Sala
Contributing Writer: Ethan Marcotte
Technical Reviewer: Brian Warren
Copy Editor: Liz Welch
Proofreader: Elle Yoko Suzuki
Compositor: David Van Ness
Indexer: Jack Lewis
Cover Designers: Dan Cederholm with Mimi Heft
Cover Production: Michael Tanamachi, shelftown

ISBN 13: 978-0-321-64338-4
ISBN 10:   0-321-64338-0

9 8 7 6 5 4 3 2 1
Printed and bound in the United States of America

For Tenley.

Acknowledgements

To Ethan Marcotte for agreeing to write an absolute gem of a chapter for the book. It's worth the cover price for his efforts alone.

To Brian Warren for being an excellent technical editor, all-around great guy, and fellow beverage aficionado.

To Rebecca Gulick for yet again making the craft of book-writing a pleasant one. I could write 1000 more books so long as Rebecca is steering the ship. You probably don't want me to write 1000 more books, but just so we're clear that it's possible because of her expertise.

To Liz Welch for going above and beyond the task of copyediting. Liz makes me sound far better than I actually do.

To Mary Sweeney for helping a video newbie and producing a great product.

To Peachpit Press and the team at New Riders for publishing this book (and DVD).

To Meagan Fisher for help with research, feedback, and owltasticness.

To the folks at An Event Apart, Web Directions, Webstock, Web Design World, @media, and other events where much of the material for this book was honed.

To the clients and customers of SimpleBits.

To Front Street Coffeehouse, Jaho Coffee & Tea, Gulu Gulu Cafe, and Fuel for providing local inspiration and caffeineation.

And lastly but most importantly, to my wife Kerry, son Jack, and daughter Tenley. I do all of this (minus the cursing) for you guys.

Contents

Introduction

Any intelligent fool can make things bigger, more complex, and more violent. It takes a touch of genius—and a lot of courage—to move in the opposite direction.

—Albert Einstein

I grew up in Vermont. And that's where my fascination with and appreciation for *craftsmanship* comes from. I can remember as a kid going with my mom to the farmers' market every Saturday morning, where all the local artists and craftspeople sold their wares out of the back of pickup trucks. The quality was tangible. You could pick it up and examine it, taste it.

Vermont has become a symbol for craftsmanship quality. The state, in a way, is a brand in and of itself. For example, in his article "The Brand Called Vermont" (http://boston.com/news/globe/ideas/articles/2003/10/12/the_brand_called_vermont), Paul Greenberg of the *Boston Globe* writes

> *A product labeled* "Made in Vermont" *—whether herb-infused maple syrup, pineapple pepper jam, or chai water buffalo yogurt—is worth 10 percent more than the same product made elsewhere.*

Why is that? I know for me, a Vermont-crafted product often conjures up an image of an old, long-bearded man up on a mountaintop, carving a dining room table out of maple. It doesn't evoke products coming off an assembly line.

NOTE

Coincidentally, Ethan Marcotte (author of the wonderful Chapter 6) also grew up in Vermont. Fist bump for the Green Mountain State.

So, when I think of craftsmanship, I tend to think that when something is well crafted, it reflects that a *human* was behind its design, a pair of hands carefully choosing the details that go into something well made and of high quality.

These details are not always obvious. With a well-made piece of furniture, you might not notice how well made it is until you start using it. Pull out the drawer and notice the dovetail joints, for instance.

All of this can be related to Web design. Seemingly nonobvious details can often separate good Web design from great Web design. You might not appreciate the quality of a well-designed website until you start using it, looking under the hood, putting it through tests.

Handcrafted CSS is an attempt to share some of the details that matter most—all in an effort to continue the flexible, bulletproof, highly efficient, and adaptable interfaces that make up a solid user experience.

What This Book Is About

Each chapter of this book contains practical examples that relate to three aspects of craftsmanship as they apply to designing with CSS: bulletproof design, progressive enrichment, and a reevaluation of past methods and best practices.

BULLETPROOF DESIGN

If you're familiar with my previous book, *Bulletproof Web Design*, you already know the benefits of designing with flexibility in mind—and the importance of planning for worst-case scenarios.

You don't need to own *Bulletproof Web Design* in order to dive into this book, but if you have read it, it'll act very much as a continuation of the core concepts covered in that book—flexibility and adaptability—using updated thinking and methods (some of which weren't available when *Bulletproof Web Design* was originally written).

In a sense, implementing designs with these bulletproof concepts is an aspect of craftsmanship. You determine how flexible a design is, or how it may adapt to varying amounts of content or text size—the sort of details that are not always obvious until you start using your design, editing it, or putting it through the rigors of everyday use.

We'll continue striving for bulletproofness in this book as well, and kick things off in Chapter 1 with a refresher on the importance of flexibility.

PROGRESSIVE ENRICHMENT

It's an exciting time to be designing for the Web! The browser landscape is changing rapidly, and browsers are implementing new and evolving standards at an increasingly faster pace. This means we can experiment with, and sometimes even *use*, these cutting-edge technologies *today*, while they're being folded into the latest browser base.

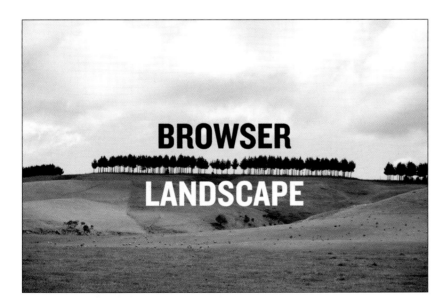

You're likely already familiar with the term "progressive enhancement" when referring to behavior and gracefully degrading JavaScript—ensuring there's a fallback when scripts are turned off or unavailable, for instance. I'll be using the term "progressive *enrichment*" when talking specifically about advanced CSS and CSS3 properties that work in forward-thinking browsers today.

We'll spend many pages discussing the future of CSS and what we can experiment with and use now. I'll show you how these advanced styles degrade beautifully, and you'll learn that websites don't have to look exactly the same in every browser.

REEVALUATION OF PAST METHODS AND BEST PRACTICES

Now, because of this rapid adoption of new standards, it's a good time to reevaluate past methods and solutions as well, and that's another theme that runs throughout the concepts in the book.

Are there new, easier, or more efficient ways to solve a particular problem that we may have used a hack or patch to solve in the past? It's important to take stock of what were previously considered best practices in order to simplify and streamline code today.

You'll find several examples in the book where we reevaluate things, investigating whether there's a better way using the current crop of browsers and their latest CSS support.

Who Is This Book For?

The pile of CSS books written to date has become a tall one. Do we really need yet another book about CSS? My hope is that for most, CSS and Web standards have become familiar and commonplace. We don't need more books covering the basics or explaining why CSS is a good thing. Instead, we can dive right into practice, solving problems with the tools we have at our disposal at the present time. And that, to me, is what makes writing a CSS book exciting.

Handcrafted CSS is for the CSS designer who wants to go the extra mile. It'll encourage crafting those details into your interfaces that elevate good design. It will also help you prepare for the future. For example, by understanding the CSS3 properties that are already being implemented by browsers, you'll have a leg up on the technology that will be helping to make our lives as Web designers easier going forward.

SOME ASSUMPTIONS

I'm making some assumptions here about you, dear reader. I assume that you're at least familiar with CSS and HTML and the concept of semantic markup and the benefits of Web standards. As I mentioned earlier, we'll jump right in, going straight into examples and dissecting our case study.

Do you have to be a CSS expert? By no means. But being familiar with basic concepts will certainly help.

HANDCRAFTED HTML?

Just as there's much happening in the CSS world regarding CSS3 and the rapid adoption of those evolving standards, there's a lot brewing in the HTML world as well. HTML5 is gaining steam as the next version of the language of the Web. And although the spec won't be finished for quite some time, browsers are already implementing portions of HTML5 right now.

There is surely still a lot to be worked out, and much of HTML5 isn't quite ready for prime time at the time of this writing. That said, for the examples in this book, we're still using the XHTML 1.0 Transitional doctype. Which is to say, the example code mentioned throughout sits inside a template that looks something like this:

```
<!DOCTYPE html PUBLIC "-//W3C//DTD XHTML 1.0 Transitional//EN"
  "http://www.w3.org/TR/xhtml1/DTD/xhtml1-transitional.dtd">
<html xmlns="http://www.w3.org/1999/xhtml" xml:lang="en"
➥lang="en">
<head>
  <meta http-equiv="content-type" content="text/html;
➥charset=utf-8" />
  <title>Tugboat Coffee Company</title>
  ...
</head>
```

> **NOTE**
>
> The announcement that the W3C would halt the XHTML2 Working Group at the end of 2009 further clarifies HTML5 as the future of markup: http://www.w3.org/News/2009#item119

(continued on next page)

```
<body>
   ... example code goes here ...
</body>
</html>
```

For now, I'm most comfortable with the *syntax* rules that go along with authoring XHTML: writing tags and attributes in lowercase, closing all elements, quotes around attribute values, etc. Regardless of the doctype I'm using in the future, I'll likely continue with that convention, as it keeps my documents clean, clear and well formed.

I'm also confident that when HTML5 reaches the tipping point in terms of browser implementation, it won't be a huge leap to convert our existing markup to the new version.

Oh, and that leaves room for a sequel to this book. :)

RESETTING STYLES

I should also mention that the examples in this book also assume that a *reset stylesheet* is used. A `reset.css` file is imported before all other stylesheets, zeroing out the default styles that are applied by most browsers. It avoids having to repeat often-used rules like `margin: 0; padding: 0;`, for instance, in multiple declarations. It also gives you a consistent base in which to apply your own styles.

I'll go into far more detail regarding `reset.css` in Chapter 5, but I just want you to be aware that resetting is in place for the examples that follow throughout the book.

TIP

For more interesting thoughts on the merits of XHTML in an HTML5 future, see http://adactio.com/journal/1595 and http://zeldman.com/2009/07/07/in-defense-of-web-developers.

Our Case Study

Throughout the book, we'll be using a template I designed for the (fictional) Tugboat Coffee Company. It's not meant to be the best interface ever designed—but rather, it has many examples baked right into it, in order to maintain a consistent example through each chapter.

You can download the template files and example code from the book's website: http://handcraftedcss.com.

So pour a cup of dark roast (or your favorite beverage) and let's start handcrafting pixels and text.

1

Always Ask, "What Happens If...?"

You can tear a poem apart to see what makes it tick.... You're back with the mystery of having been moved by words. The best craftsmanship always leaves holes and gaps...so that something that is not in the poem can creep, crawl, flash or thunder in.

—Dylan Thomas, *Poetic Manifesto*, 1961

Dylan Thomas was a poet writing in the context of mid-twentieth-century Welsh society, but his thoughts on craftsmanship could be applied to just about anything, including our wonderful and complex profession of designing for the Web. Leaving room for unanticipated use is a thread that runs throughout the concept of being "bulletproof," and in this chapter, we'll reintroduce the topic by deconstructing a simple list of links found in the sidebar of our case study.

Often the decisions we make as designers and design implementers directly reflect the integrity of the interface. What happens if there is more (or less) content on the page than planned? What happens if the text size of the page increases or decreases? What happens if there are two paragraphs instead of one? And what if one of those paragraphs is translated into, say, German?

Flexibility in Web design is the mark of a true craftsman. Designing something statically in an image editor is one achievement, but allowing for give and take within the boundaries of a page layout is what sets good Web design apart from great Web design. It's taking the Web *as a medium* into account as part of the design process, and letting go of pixel precision.

Let's take a look at one quick example that illustrates bulletproof design in the Tugboat template, where we'll channel our "inner Dylan," letting the possibility for future things to creep, crawl, flash, or thunder in.

A Simple List of Links

If we take a look at the Tugboat template (**Figure 1.1**), we're going to zero in on the little "Drink Menu" module in the top right of the sidebar (**Figure 1.2**). It's a common design pattern: a vertical list of clickable items, each with some meta-information aligned to the right (in this case the price of each drink). A subtle horizontal rule separates each row of data.

Figure 1.2

Figure 1.1 Tugboat Coffee Company: The fictional case study we'll be using throughout the book.

Ten bucks for a Caramel Macchiato! I know, I know, but by the time this book hits the shelves, it's entirely possible.

Block-Level Links

Now the first thing we want to ensure is that the entire row (link title *and* price) is clickable, not just the drink name itself. This increases usability and makes for a nicer user experience, with a nice, fat clickable area. It enables us to add a hover effect to the row, while allowing the reader to select the link without obscuring the text (**Figure 1.3**).

By increasing the clickable area, we're applying Fitts' Law. Paul Fitts was an American psychologist who is famous for this principle: "The time to acquire a target is a function of the distance to and size of the target." In other words, the larger the target, the quicker and easier it is to get there. Pretty sensible, especially when applied to interface design. Now let's dive into the code that'll make this happen.

DRINK MENU	
Latte	2.79
Cappuccino	2.99
Cafe Americano	1.80
Espresso	2.00
Caramel Macchiato	10.49

Figure 1.3 The entire row is clickable, not just the blue link text.

TIP

For more on Fitts' Law as it relates to hyperlinks, see http://www.uie.com/brainsparks/2008/02/28/usability-tools-podcast-applying-fittss-law/, http://www.1976design.com/blog/archive/2004/09/07/link-presentation-fitts-law/, and http://www.mezzoblue.com/archives/2004/08/19/fitts_law/.

THE MARKUP

Since it's a list of items, let's use a simple unordered list to mark up each row, wrapping the price in its own element so that we can position it over to the right.

```
<ul class="lst">
  <li><a href="/drinks/latte">Latte <em>2.79</em></a></li>
  <li><a href="/drinks/capp">Cappucino <em>2.99</em></a></li>
  <li><a href="/drinks/amer">Cafe Americano <em>1.80</em>
➥</a></li>
  <li><a href="/drinks/espr">Espresso <em>2.00</em></a></li>
  <li><a href="/drinks/carm">Carmel Macchiato <em>10.49</em>
➥</a></li>
</ul>
```

You'll notice I'm using an `<em>` element to wrap around the price, but any inline element (`<span>`, `<strong>`, etc.) would work fine here as well.

NOTE

We need to choose an inline element (<span>, <strong>, etc.) rather than a block-level element (<div>, <h2>, etc.) here because we're inside an <a> element, which itself is an inline element. In other words, block-level elements can't live inside inline elements.

SETTING THE LINK STYLE

Let's start by declaring a global style for links across the template, making them blue and bold with no underline by default.

```
a:link {
  font-weight: bold;
  text-decoration: none;
  color: #3792b3;
  }
```

DRINK MENU

Latte *2.79*

Cappuccino *2.99*

Cafe Americano *1.80*

Espresso *2.00*

Caramel Macchiato *10.49*

Figure 1.4

Next, in order to enable Fitts' Law, we'll want to make the links inside each list item *block-level* with CSS so that they'll span the entire width of the list. We'll also add some padding and a bottom border (**Figure 1.4**).

```
ul.lst li a {
    display: block;
    padding: 7px;
    border-bottom: 1px solid #f3f2e8;
    }
```

STYLING THE PRICE

We'll now want to add a declaration that styles the price. Since most browsers italicize text within <em> elements, we'll want to set that back to normal, set the font-weight to normal, and change the color (since our default style for links is blue and bold).

```
ul.lst li em {
    font-style: normal;
    font-weight: normal;
    color: #9c836e;
    }
```

DRINK MENU

Latte 2.79

Cappuccino 2.99

Cafe Americano 1.80

Espresso 2.00

Caramel Macchiato 10.49

Figure 1.5

Figure 1.5 shows the styled price that's now sitting just to the right of each drink text. And now we're getting closer.

POSITIONING THE PRICE

Now we can position the price over to the right. Let's try using *absolute positioning* here, specifying coordinates in relation to whatever row the price is in. To do that, we'll need to first declare each link as position: relative;. Then we can position each price within that link 7 pixels from the top right (equal to the amount of padding we have around each link).

```
ul.lst li a {
    position: relative;
    display: block;
    padding: 7px;
    border-bottom: 1px solid #f3f2e8;
    }
```

```
ul.lst li em {
  position: absolute;
  top: 7px;
  right: 7px;
  font-style: normal;
  font-weight: normal;
  color: #9c836e;
  }
```

Figure 1.6 shows the finished list, with the price positioned over to the right in a different font treatment than the drink title, all the while keeping the entire row a clickable hyperlink. Cheers to us. But now let's talk about what can go wrong with the way we've implemented things.

Figure 1.6

Unintentional Overlap

Remember when our friend Dylan Thomas wrote about good craftsmanship leaving holes and gaps so that something unforeseen could slide in? Taking our current list treatment to task, we can quickly see how things can break down when combining absolute positioning with varying lengths of content.

Our list with the current titles and prices in place looks perfectly fine, but what happens when a drink name goes beyond a few words?

You'll notice in **Figure 1.7** that with a longer drink title, in this case my favorite "Half-caf, non-fat, triple-shot latte (with a twist of lemon)," we get an awful overlap of the title and its positioned price.

Figure 1.7

When we use absolute positioning, we take that element out of the normal flow of the document, and if we're not careful, collisions can happen, where overlapping content becomes unreadable. In some cases, the overlap is what you want to have happen; therefore, absolute positioning is your friend. But here, we're dealing with two varying bits of hypertext, and collisions are not what we're after (cue sad trombone).

But we're craftspeople of the Web! Great craftspeople know to *look ahead*, asking questions along the way, such as, "What happens if the drink title is longer and wraps to two lines?" By asking that question, we're improving the flexibility and integrity of the design. This is great Web design.

What Happens if Text Size Is Adjusted?

Another question we need to ask is, what happens when readers adjust the text size in their browsers? Even with the initial shorter drink titles, we could still run into trouble if the text is increased two notches above a normal, default size.

DRINK MENU

Latte	2.79
Cappuccino	2.99
Cafe Americano	1.80
Espresso	2.00
Caramel Macchia10.049	

Figure 1.8 Showing the list with the text size increased two notches above the browser's default medium setting.

Figure 1.8 shows another overlapping scenario, with the previously short-enough "Caramel Macchiato" now overlapping its price at a larger text size.

Great Web design accounts for these scenarios. When we're implementing design, it's important to consider that content may shift during flight. Amounts, sizes, and placement of hypertext may change, flow differently, and render slightly smaller or larger than originally intended. That's okay. By anticipating these adjustments, we can make sure the design doesn't break down. This is what we refer to as "bulletproof design," and it's a characteristic of good craftsmanship on the Web.

It's the kind of detail that isn't obvious. It's not flashy or pretty—but it's a crucial aspect of designing for the Web. Let's apply some *bulletproofness* to this list example, paving the way for varying lengths of content.

Guessing at Content Length

One improvement we could make here to prevent overlap is to increase the right padding of the link enough until the overlap is gone.

DRINK MENU

Latte	2.79
Cappuccino	2.99
Cafe Americano	1.80
Espresso	2.00
Half-caf, non-fat, triple-shot latte (with a twist of lemon)	10.49

Figure 1.9   50px

```
ul.lst li a {
  position: relative;
  display: block;
  padding: 7px 50px 7px 7px;
  border-bottom: 1px solid #f3f2e8;
}
```

Increasing the right padding to 50px from 7px yields the result in **Figure 1.9**, which shows the title wrapping before overlapping the price. I chose 50px after several attempts, until there was enough space on the right to clear the price. In other words, currently the price's width never exceeds 50 pixels.

The problem with this approach is that we're guessing at what the content length might be. For instance, 50px might be enough space on the right today, but as soon as coffee prices jump to over $100 (oh, and they will) we'll get overlap once again. Also, if the text size increases, 50px quickly becomes an irrelevant number to measure against, since the price could easily expand beyond that.

A SITUATION WHERE ABSOLUTE POSITIONING MAKES GOOD SENSE

There is a scenario in which using absolute positioning is a perfectly fine option. Let's say that instead of text-based price, we were positioning a *graphic* of some kind. An image has finite dimensions, and we could plug in whatever maximum width it had as right padding to the drink title.

Figure 1.10 shows our drink list with star rating GIFs (from 1 to 4 stars) instead of price. We'll still wrap each star image in the <em> element for positioning, just as we did for the price.

```
<ul class="lst">
  <li><a href="/drinks/latte">Latte <em><img src="/img/
➥stars-3.gif" alt="3/4 stars" /></em></a></li>
  <li><a href="/drinks/capp">Cappuccino <em><img src="/img/
➥stars-2.gif" alt="2/4 stars" /></em></a></li>
  <li><a href="/drinks/amer">Cafe Americano <em><img src=
➥"/img/stars-4.gif" alt="4/4 stars" /></em></a></li>
  <li><a href="/drinks/espr">Espresso <em><img src=
➥"/img/stars-1.gif" alt="1/4 stars" /></em></a></li>
  <li><a href="/drinks/trip">Half-caf, non-fat, triple-shot
➥latte (with a twist of lemon) <em><img src="/img/stars-3.
➥gif" alt="3/4 stars" /></em></a></li>
</ul>
```

The width of each image is 57 pixels. With that known amount, we can safely apply the right amount of padding to the link that will never change (57px + a little more for spacing):

```
ul.lst li a {
  position: relative;
  display: block;
  padding: 7px 60px 7px 7px;
  border-bottom: 1px solid #f3f2e8;
  }
```

Using *em* units for padding would be a better choice here, as that calculated width would scale along with the text size (e.g., padding: 7px 4em 7px 7px;)

Figure 1.10

So, for elements that are of fixed-width dimensions (images, for example) or in situations where you're certain of content size, absolute positioning makes for an easy-to-implement solution. However, for elements that may vary in length or amount, floating continues to be our best option, which is what we'll tackle next.

Improving Flexibility with Float

Instead of using absolute positioning to place the drink price over to the right, let's instead use float, which will enable a bit of flexibility and avoid the overlapping posed by using absolute positioning.

A NEW MARKUP ORDER

We'll need to make a small tweak to the markup in order for a simple float to work. Let's put the <em> element that's wrapped around price *before* the drink title.

You could argue that this is nonoptimal ordering, and that the price should come after the drink title. Or you could argue that the price should come *before* the drink title, even though we're displaying the opposite. Regardless, it's one of the reasons I like using <em> or <strong> in these cases. If screen-reading software reads this aloud, there will be a differential in the way each is read (faster, louder), thus giving some separation to the content.

If the order presented here isn't sitting well with you, fear not. We'll talk about a way of reversing that in just a bit.

```
<ul class="lst">
  <li><a href="/drinks/latte"><em>2.79</em> Latte</a></li>
  <li><a href="/drinks/capp"><em>2.99</em> Cappuccino</a>
➥</li>
  <li><a href="/drinks/amer"><em>1.80</em> Cafe Americano
➥</a></li>
  <li><a href="/drinks/espr"><em>2.00</em> Espresso</a></li>
  <li><a href="/drinks/trip"><em>10.49</em> Half-caf,
➥non-fat, triple-shot
    latte (with a twist of lemon)</a></li>
</ul>
```

FLOATING THE PRICE

Now that we've swapped the order, putting the price before the drink, we can float the price to the right, rather that absolutely positioning it. I've removed the previous rules that handled the absolute positioning.

```
ul.lst li a {
  position: relative;
  display: block;
  padding: 7px;
```

```
    border-bottom: 1px solid #f3f2e8;
    }
ul.lst li em {
    position: absolute;
    top: 7px;
    right: 7px;
    float: right;
    font-style: normal;
    font-weight: normal;
    color: #9c836e;
    }
```

Figure 1.11

Pretty simple, right? Just applying the float property to the price positions it over to the right where we want it. But it also means that the price and title will be aware of each other, never overlapping (**Figure 1.11**).

We can sleep well at night, knowing that this little list of drinks will now be able to accommodate any length title the crafty baristas can come up with.

PASSING THE TEXT SIZE TEST

We can also give it a quick integrity test by bumping up the text size a few notches. **Figure 1.12** shows that when using a float for the price, a text size increase will not affect the readability of the list.

Figure 1.12

A More Optimal Markup Order

Don't like the price coming before the drink title in the markup? There's a solution, and it involves using *opposing floats*. By floating the drink title left and the price right, we can order the markup more optimally. We'll just need to wrap the title itself in an element so that we can apply a float to it as well.

I'm going to choose the wonderfully generic <span> element in this case, but you could use any inline element you'd like here (e.g., <strong>).

```
<ul class="lst">
  <li><a href="/drinks/latte"><span>Latte</span> <em>2.79
➥</em></a></li>
  <li><a href="/drinks/capp"><span>Cappuccino</span> <em>
➥2.99</em></a></li>
```
(continued on next page)

```
    <li><a href="/drinks/amer"><span>Cafe Americano</span>
⇒<em>1.80</em></a></li>
    <li><a href="/drinks/espr"><span>Espresso</span> <em>2.00
⇒</em></a></li>
    <li><a href="/drinks/trip"><span>Half-caf, non-fat,
⇒triple-shot
      latte (with a twist of lemon)</span> <em>10.49</em></a>
⇒</li>
</ul>
```

With both the title and price wrapped in their own elements, we can now apply the opposing floats that will align things the way we'd like:

```
ul.lst li a {
  display: block;
  padding: 7px;
  border-bottom: 1px solid #f3f2e8;
  overflow: hidden;
  }
ul.lst li span {
  float: left;
  }
ul.lst li em {
  float: right;
  font-style: normal;
  font-weight: normal;
  color: #9c836e;
  }
```

```
DRINK MENU

Latte                            2.79

Cappuccino                       2.99

Cafe Americano                   1.80

Espresso                         2.00

Half-caf, non-fat, triple-shot
latte (with a twist of lemon)
                                10.49
```

Figure 1.13

Figure 1.13 shows the results. You'll notice that we've added `overflow: hidden;` to the `<a>` element that encloses the floating `<span>` and `<em>` element. This is one method of self-clearing any floats that occur within the containing element. Each row will remain independent, with the floats from one row not affecting the others around it. There's more on modular float containment in Chapter 6.

You'll also notice while there is no overlapping, the price is dropping below the drink title on the last item. When a floated element doesn't have a specific width specified, it'll expand as wide as it can. Since this title is longer than the others, it's expanding the full width, pushing the price down below it.

SPECIFYING A WIDTH FOR FLOATED ELEMENTS

To fix this, we'll need to specify a width to the drink titles. And we'll have to do so by taking a guess at content length, just as we did in the absolute positioning method. The difference here, though, is that while our guess might be off in future scenarios, we'll never get an unreadable overlap; we'll just get the price falling down below the title. Visually, it's not what we want, but ensuring readability *is* an advantage here.

One simple way to add a width to the title is by using a percentage. Let's add width: 75%; to the <span> element that's floating left. By using a percentage, we'll have a better chance of avoiding collision with the price should the width of the surrounding box or general layout of the page change in the future (and by *collision*, again we're talking about the price bumping down below the title and not overlapping, which would happen if using absolute positioning).

```
ul.lst li a {
  display: block;
  padding: 7px;
  border-bottom: 1px solid #f3f2e8;
  overflow: hidden;
  }
ul.lst li span {
  float: left;
  width: 75%;
  }
ul.lst li em {
  float: right;
  font-style: normal;
  font-weight: normal;
  color: #9c836e;
  }
```

```
DRINK MENU

Latte                        2.79

Cappuccino                   2.99

Cafe Americano               1.80

Espresso                     2.00

Half-caf, non-fat,          10.49
triple-shot latte (with
a twist of lemon)
```

Figure 1.14 shows the longer drink title wrapping because it now has a width of 75% applied. And with that, we have a flexible system for showing drink titles and prices.

Figure 1.14

How About a Table?

You might be saying something like, "But, Dan, what about using a <table> to mark this list up?" And you'd have a good argument there. While the <table> has been rightly banished for *layout* purposes, there's no reason it couldn't be used for what it was originally intended: *tabular data*. You could also argue that, as simple as it is, this list of drink titles and their associated prices is in fact tabular data and could be marked up as such.

I always say that there are approximately 3,296 ways to achieve the same result in Web design. And this little module we've been dealing with throughout the chapter is no exception.

Here's how we might mark this example up as a table, with each of the drink titles as table headers, and the price as table cells:

```html
<table>
  <tr>
    <th><a href="/drinks/latte">Latte</a></th>
    <td>2.79</td>
  </tr>
  <tr>
    <th><a href="/drinks/capp">Cappuccino</a></th>
    <td>2.99</td>
  </tr>
  <tr>
    <th><a href="/drinks/amer">Cafe Americano</a></th>
    <td>1.80</td>
  </tr>
  <tr>
    <th><a href="/drinks/espr">Espresso</a></th>
    <td>2.00</td>
  </tr>
  <tr>
    <th><a href="/drinks/trip">Half-caf, non-fat,
triple-shot lutte (with a twist of lemon)</a></th>
    <td>10.49</td>
  </tr>
</table>
```

LINKS AROUND BLOCK-LEVEL ELEMENTS

I've chosen to link only the drink title, but therein lies the problem: a hyperlink can't wrap a block-level element, so we'd have no easy way of making the entire row clickable like we had using a list. In other words, if it was kosher to wrap each `<th>` and `<td>` with an `<a>` element, we could achieve the same results. But currently, it's not possible.

As a theoretical illustration, here's what I mean by wrapping the hyperlink around the block-level `<th>` and `<td>` elements, which is currently unsupported/invalid:

```
<table>
  <tr>
    <a href="/drinks/latte">
      <th>Latte</th>
      <td>2.79</td>
    </a>
  </tr>
  <tr>
    <a href="/drinks/capp">
      <th>Cappuccino</th>
      <td>2.99</td>
    </a>
  </tr>
  <tr>
    <a href="/drinks/amer">
      <th>Cafe Americano</th>
      <td>1.80</td>
    </a>
  </tr>
  <tr>
    <a href="/drinks/espr">
      <th>Espresso</th>
      <td>2.00</td>
    </a>
  </tr>
  <tr>
    <a href="/drinks/trip">
      <th>Half-caf, non-fat, triple-shot latte (with a twist
➥of lemon)</th>
      <td>10.49</td>
```

(continued on next page)

NOTE

Allowing the `<a>` element to surround multiple elements and block-level elements is something that might be coming in HTML 5 (http://www.brucelawson.co.uk/2008/any-element-linking-in-html-5/). And boy, wouldn't that be nice?

```
    </a>
  </tr>
</table>
```

So, for the sake of user experience, and the fact that this is a very simple list with two pieces of data, we'll opt to stick to an unordered list with clickable rows.

Adding Data Visualization

For extra fun, why not add some data visualization to the list of drink titles and prices? Since we're already dealing with vertical, clickable rows of data, it wouldn't be too difficult to add some underlying bar graphs to the list, further accenting the difference between the items in the list.

In our case, we'd be visualizing the difference in price, but you could see how bar graphs could be applied to other vertical lists as well—for example, a vertical list of article categories, with the number of articles in each category floated right. A bar graph background behind the category and number could visualize the difference in those amounts. It's a nice way of scanning the list to instantly grasp the comparison.

Figure 1.15 shows how bar graph backgrounds could be added to Tugboat's drink list, with the width of the bar relating to its associated price. This technique is explained by Wilson Miner in an article published at A List Apart ("Accessible Data Visualization with Web Standards," http://www.alistapart.com/articles/accessibledatavisualization). Wilson explains how to add rich data visualization by using best practices in CSS, and the bar graph example is one of many excellent examples.

Let's quickly walk through the steps required to add in this extra bit of scannable usefulness to the drink list example we've been working with throughout the chapter.

DRINK MENU	
Latte	2.79
Cappuccino	2.99
Cafe Americano	1.80
Espresso	2.00
Caramel Macchiato	10.49

Figure 1.15

ADDING DATA TO THE MARKUP

Our markup will change slightly in order to add the bar graph information. Essentially, we'll want to add a percentage value that corresponds to the width of each bar. We'll be setting that percentage against the largest price. In other words, the largest price in the list will equal 100%, and all the others will be a percentage lower based off that.

```
<ul class="lst">
  <li><a href="/drinks/latte"><em>2.79</em> Latte</a>
➥<span>60%</span></li>
  <li><a href="/drinks/capp"><em>2.99</em> Cappuccino</a>
➥<span>68%</span></li>
  <li><a href="/drinks/amer"><em>1.80</em> Cafe Americano
➥</a> <span>35%</span></li>
  <li><a href="/drinks/espr"><em>2.00</em> Espresso</a>
➥<span>50%</span></li>
  <li><a href="/drinks/carm"><em>10.49</em> Carmel Macchiato
➥</a> <span>100%</span></li>
</ul>
```

We now have the extra data in the markup: a percentage based on the largest price equaling 100%. I've chosen to use a generic `<span>` element here, and place it outside the `<a>`.

NOTE

I've taken guesses at the actual percentages for demonstration purposes. A backend system would likely do the heavy lifting here in terms of working out the math.

APPLYING BASE STYLES

With the markup set, let's now reapply those base styles to get the block-level links working, with the price floated over to the right again.

```
ul.lst li {
  margin: 0 0 2px 0;
  }
ul.lst li a {
  display: block;
  padding: 7px;
  }
ul.lst li em {
  float: right;
  font-style: normal;
  font-weight: normal;
  color: #9c836e;
  }
```

Figure 1.16 shows the results, where as you can see, the percentage is now hanging out down below the title and price.

What we actually want is a bar graph representing that percentage displayed behind the clickable row, and not the percentage text itself. So, on to something crafty.

Figure 1.16

HIDING THE PERCENTAGE TEXT AND CREATING THE BAR

Next we'll hide the percentage text that's currently showing, giving the `<span>` a height, width, and background, and then position it *behind* its clickable row. While the data is correct in the markup, we'll use CSS to hide it and turn it into a bar graph.

Our first step is to add a width to each `<span>`. We could create class names for each width we need, but the easiest approach is to add the width to the markup as an inline style. Adding style attributes to the markup is not something I'd normally encourage; however, typically it's going to be a backend process that calculates the width, and having that split out in the markup is the easiest way to handle it. In this case, having that tiny bit of inline style is rather harmless. In fact, you could argue that it's actually more in the spirit of keeping content and style separate when specifying the width inline. It's almost as if the backend process is creating an "image" with this code.

```
<ul class="lst">
  <li><a href="/drinks/latte"><em>2.79</em> Latte</a> <span
➥style="width: 60%;">60%</span></li>
  <li><a href="/drinks/capp"><em>2.99</em> Cappuccino</a>
➥<span style="width: 68%;">68%</span></li>
  <li><a href="/drinks/amer"><em>1.80</em> Cafe Americano</a>
➥<span style="width: 35%;">35%</span></li>
  <li><a href="/drinks/espr"><em>2.00</em> Espresso</a>
➥<span style="width: 50%;">50%</span></li>
  <li><a href="/drinks/carm"><em>10.49</em> Carmel Macchiato
➥</a> <span style="width: 100%;">100%</span></li>
</ul>
```

Now let's add the styles that do the real magic here. In this case, we actually *want* overlap to happen—that is, the link text overlapping the bar graph as a background. So, we'll use absolute positioning to make that happen (yet another scenario where it makes good sense). Our first step is to add `position: relative;` to both the `<li>` and the `<a>` elements so that the coordinates of each bar graph will be placed inside their respective rows.

```
ul.lst li {
  position: relative;
  margin: 0 0 2px 0;
  }
ul.lst li a {
  position: relative;
```

```
  display: block;
  padding: 7px;
  }
ul.lst li em {
  float: right;
  font-style: normal;
  font-weight: normal;
  color: #9c836e;
  }
```

Next, we'll add the declaration to style and position the <span> that will create the bar graph:

```
ul.lst li span {
  position: absolute;
  top: 0;
  left: 0;
  display: block;
  height: 100%;
  text-indent: -9999px;
  background: #f3f2e8;
  }
```

There are several important things taking place in this little declaration. Along with positioning the bar graph top and left, since <span> is an inline element, we'll switch that to display: block; and add height: 100%; to have it fill the entire height of the row. We're also using text-indent: -9999px; to shove the percentage text way, way off to the left to completely hide it. It's still there for screen-reading software and other devices, but it's not visible on the page. We added a light tan background color as well so that the text will still be legible on top of it.

Stacking order problem

Figure 1.17 shows where we are currently, and as you can see, things look pretty good, except for the bar graph sitting on top and obscuring the title and price. To fix this stacking order issue, we'll add a bit of z-index magic to pull the title and price over the graph.

z-index is a CSS property that allows you to adjust the stacking order of positioned elements, and by adding z-index: 2; to the link, we're giving it higher priority than the bar graph, which will now sit behind it.

Figure 1.17

Figure 1.18

```
ul.lst li a {
    position: relative;
    display: block;
    padding: 7px;
    z-index: 2;
}
```

With the `z-index` fix in place, we have a finished list, with the bar graphs displaying correctly behind the title and price (**Figure 1.18**).

Adding a hover treatment

We could also add a hover treatment, changing the background color of the bar graph when the user hovers over the row with the mouse. Since the bar graph is outside the link in the markup, we can still achieve a background color swap by attaching the hover state to the `<li>` instead.

```
ul.lst li:hover span {
    background: #ecebe1;
}
```

Figure 1.19 shows how the bar graph will change color when hovered over, as a result of the declaration we've just added. This won't work in Microsoft Internet Explorer 6, but that's okay. In this case, I'm fine with there being no hover change in IE6. There are, however, other more important issues in IE6 that we'll need to tackle in order for the bar graphs to render properly. Let's do that now.

Figure 1.19

FIXING THINGS IN INTERNET EXPLORER 6

Figure 1.20 shows how our current markup and style for the drink list with the bar graph renders in IE6. Not perfect by any means, as you can see. Typically, like a lot of you, I'll code in Safari or Firefox; get things looking right with clean, standards-based code; then open up in IE6, weep, and fix. Repeat. Fortunately for this particular example, things aren't *too* bad, and with a few little fixes we'll have it working just like all the other browsers in no time.

Figure 1.20 There are a few problems with our list, as displayed here in IE6.

There are a few problems to note here:

- There is too much vertical space between each row.

- The bar graph isn't filling the entire height of the row.

- The bar graph is overlapping the price (but not the drink title).

We can fix two of the three problems quickly by adding the magical and mystical `height: 1%;` trick to both the `<li>` and the `<a>`. This hack will tighten the list back up as well as fix the bar graph-overlapping-price problem.

While we want IE6 to apply the hack, we don't want other browsers to see it. So, we'll preface the rules with `* html`, which is a handy way of targeting CSS to IE6 and IE6 only.

```
* html ul.lst li,
* html ul.lst li a {
  height: 1%;
  }
```

Figure 1.21 shows the progress, where we've added the `height: 1%;` trick to the list items and links to tighten up the list and fix the price overlap issue in IE6.

Finally, we need to stretch the height of the background bar graph to fill the entire height of the row. We're already specifying a height of 100% on the `<span>`, yet IE6 is not playing nice. Wouldn't be the first time. So, as an extra measure, we'll use `line-height` to get things looking the way we want:

```
ul.lst li span {
  position: absolute;
  top: 0;
  left: 0;
  display: block;
  height: 100%;
  line-height: 2.55em;
  text-indent: -9999px;
  background: #f3f2e8;
  }
```

Figure 1.21 Vertical spacing is better but still not perfect here in IE6.

Figure 1.22

I landed on 2.55em by trial and error, until the background was full height. This rule is for the benefit of IE6, but it's harmless for other browsers, so this time, instead of targeting IE6 with a hack (or conditional comment), we just added the rule to the main declaration for all browsers.

Figure 1.22 shows the finished example, now working in both IE6 and IE7.

Choosing the Right Solution

We've just explored several solutions to the same problem, noting the potential problems and pitfalls that might occur. If the markup order doesn't bother you, then simply floating the price to the right (while it comes before the title in the markup) is the easiest, most flexible solution. If dealing with images, then absolute positioning might be the best option, as having a known width makes it simple to avoid overlap. And we can also look toward the future, when hyperlinking multiple block-level elements can make situations like these not only easier, but potentially more semantically sound as well.

What's important to take away here, is that by asking questions along the way, we can strengthen the integrity of our designs. The flexibility that's gained is not only bulletproof but also a characteristic of craftsmanship: that we care enough to let unanticipated scenarios affect what we've created, even when the steps we take to get there aren't inherently obvious.

We'll continue to dissect other parts of the Tugboat template with the same curiosity and critical thinking. We'll also explore when it's okay to push the envelope a bit, and start using advanced CSS3 properties now. Let's get to it. But first, another triple-shot latte is in order, no?

2

Rounded Corners with border-radius

You have to roll up your sleeves and be a stonecutter before you can become a sculptor—command of craft always precedes art: apprentice, journeyman, master.

—Philip Gerard, author

I have a bold prediction to make here, folks: Rounded corners are destined to become the hottest *new* design trend on the Web!

Rimshot

I kid, of course. But no one can deny the popularity (and more importantly the utility) of rounded corners, and that they have their place among other tools of design. And remember, it's not rounded corners that are the problem—it's the *abuse* of rounded corners that's the problem. That said, a corner that is rounded off is simply a method of manipulating a square box. It's a tool and a treatment that will always be a part of certain designs.

But *implementing* rounded corners has always been a bit of a chore. We have historically been *stonecutters*, haven't we? We've been manually inserting extra markup and carving out color palette–specific images to achieve what should be a simple code instruction—and one that would be better created entirely with CSS.

In this chapter, we're going to attack the concept of rounding corners by looking to CSS3 properties that we can begin using *today*. It's exciting and incredibly freeing to experiment with advanced CSS that previously felt decades away from real-world use. Fortunately, we have stonecutting experience under our belt. We fully understand the hard way. And as Philip Gerard said in the opening quote, you have to roll up your sleeves before becoming a sculptor.

Well, my fellow crafters, it's time to start sculpting.

We've exercised command of craft by achieving rounded corners the hard way—but now it's time to start embracing the future, reevaluating past methods, and making things a little easier on ourselves. Good craftsmanship is about understanding the various ways to solve a particular problem, then choosing the right task for the job. Let's talk about pushing the envelope just a bit, using some advanced CSS that will be yet another tool for the designer's workbench.

But first, let's go over current methods to gain some perspective on how much easier life can be.

Past and Present Rounding

You'll notice rounded corners are used in several places on the Tugboat template (**Figure 2.1**): the box surrounding the Find a Location form, the Drink Menu module, as well as the frames around each of This Week's Specials.

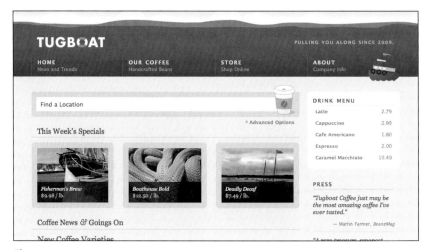

Figure 2.1

Now historically, you might've tackled this by creating a few images to overlay as background images on top of a square box. If the box's width is fixed, then you might be able to get by with creating two images (one for the top-left and top-right corners and one for the bottom-left and bottom-right corners).

Let's quickly walk through a refresher on how you can create fixed and fluid-width rounded boxes using current methods. Then we'll get into the fun stuff.

SLICING UP A FIXED-WIDTH ROUNDED BOX

Figure 2.2 shows how you can carve up a fixed-width box that's 226 pixels wide. A `round-top.gif` is used as a background image to round off the top half of the box, while a `round-bottom.gif` is used to round off the bottom half. The non-rounded portion of the box can be filled in with a background color.

> **NOTE**
>
> I'm going to be intentionally general with the following code, as my goal is to re-familiarize you with the techniques and how they work but not spend too much time walking through older solutions.

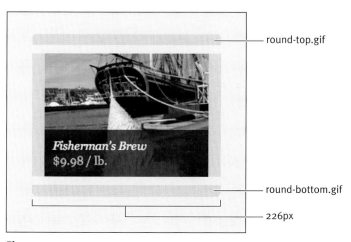

round-top.gif

round-bottom.gif

226px

Figure 2.2

This method also requires wrapping the boat image with at least two elements. Since the CSS2.1 spec allows only a single background image attached to any one element, let's add extra markup around the photo to act as hooks for those styles:

```
<div class="box">
  <div class="box-inner">
    <img src="boat.jpg" alt="boat" />
  </div>
</div>
```

Then, the CSS that positions each background image looks something like this:

```
.box {
  width: 226px;
  background: #e2e1d4 url(round-bottom.gif) no-repeat bottom
left;
  }
```

(continued on next page)

```
.box-inner {
  padding: 15px;
  background: url(round-top.gif) no-repeat top left;
}
```

The background color needs to be set on the outermost `<div class="box">`. If set on the inner `<div class="box-inner">`, it would overlap and obscure the bottom image. And the padding inside the box needs to be set on the inner `<div class="box-inner">`, so that the top image can span the entire width and meet the edges of the box (see **Figure 2.3**).

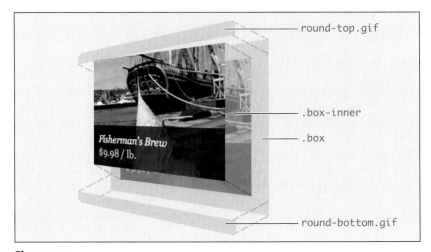

Figure 2.3

If you've implemented rounded-corner boxes in the past, this should all seem familiar. It's certainly not terrible to have to add an extra `<div>` to accommodate the second background image, and this technique works well cross-browser. But it does require the box being of a fixed width.

SLICING UP A FLUID-WIDTH ROUNDED BOX

If the box is fluid—or if you don't want to lock yourself down to a specific width—then you have to create *four* images (one for each corner). At the same time, you need *four containing elements* in order to reference each corner background image.

Figure 2.4 shows how you can carve up the four separate images: `round-tl.gif`, `round-tr.gif`, `round-bl.gif`, and `round-br.gif` —one for each corner.

Figure 2.4 Showing four separate corner images that might be laid on top of a square box.

The markup can be structured in a variety of ways, with at least four elements surrounding the image so that each of the four corners can be referenced as a background image. Let's use <div>s for the following example:

```
<div class="box">
  <div class="box-inner">
    <div class="box-inner2">
      <div class="box-inner3">
        <img src="boat.jpg" alt="boat" />
      </div>
    </div>
  </div>
</div>
```

The CSS required to turn those four elements into a fluid rounded box looks like this:

```
.box {
  background: #e2e1d4 url(round-br.gif) no-repeat bottom
right;
  }
.box-inner {
  background: url(round-bl.gif) no-repeat bottom left;
  }
.box-inner2 {
  background: url(round-tl.gif) no-repeat top left;
  }
```

(continued on next page)

```
.box-inner3 {
  padding: 15px;
  background: url(round-tr.gif) no-repeat top right;
}
```

TIP

See Simon Willison's article, "Rounded Corners with CSS and JavaScript," for an example of how to get fluid rounded boxes working with JavaScript and DOM (http://www.sitepoint.com/article/rounded-corners-css-javascript/).

Just as with the fixed-width version, the background color needs to be attached to the outermost <div>, while the padding must be specified on the innermost <div>.

Seems kind of an absurd way of achieving a rounded box, doesn't it?

Now, there are certainly other methods for achieving fluid-width rounded boxes. For example, you can use JavaScript to *dynamically* create the extra markup required as well as handle the placement of the four images. That keeps the markup minimal but requires JavaScript to be turned on in order for the rounded treatment to appear.

TIED TO A PALETTE AND A RADIUS

There are a few additional downsides to all of the aforementioned solutions. For example, if images are required, then the color of the rounded box or background that it sits on becomes a permanent decision. That is, if the colors are changed, new images must be created to match.

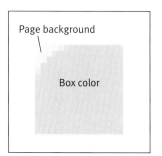

Figure 2.5 A zoomed view of a rounded corner image on top of a pre-determined page background color that will mask a square corner behind it.

The rounded images often obscure the square corners by overlaying the page background color on top of the box (**Figure 2.5**). This creates a maintenance annoyance should the colors be changed after the images are created.

The amount of roundness is also something that must be decided along with a color palette. The radius of the rounded corner is part of the image, and changing that curve involves carving out new images each time you or your client or boss changes their mind.

In short, rounded corners are labor-intensive, inflexible beasts. I probably don't need to remind you of this. But there's a better way... a new way.

The border-radius Property

CSS3 offers us the promise of applying rounded corners to any element by way of the border-radius property. Creating rounded corners couldn't be simpler, eliminating the need for any images or extra markup. Also, color and amount of roundness can be changed on the fly just by updating a few lines of CSS.

Here's a brief demonstration of how the `border-radius` property works. Using our previous example, the markup could be as simple as this:

```
<div class="box">
  <img src="boat.jpg" alt="boat" />
</div>
```

And here's the CSS to make this box round on all four corners:

```
.box {
  padding: 15px;
  background: #e2e1d4;
  border-radius: 8px;
  }
```

That declaration adds a 8px radius to each corner, clipping the background color that we've specified for the box—all through the magic of CSS. Done.

We can adjust the background color or radius amount in seconds, changing the box's appearance with a few simple rules.

Now, because this is part of the *CSS3* Working Draft (**Figure 2.6**) (http://www.w3.org/TR/css3-background/#the-border-radius), perhaps we'll be able to use this newfangled property in say, 10 years?

Well, luckily, for some browsers we don't have to wait that long. In fact, there are ways of using `border-radius` *right now*. Let's take a look.

Figure 2.6 The `border-radius` Working Draft at the W3C.

Vendor-Specific Extensions

CSS provides vendor-specific extensions; in this way, a browser vendor can create their own, proprietary properties by prefixing a property name with an extension of their organization.

Often, this is a way for the browser vendor to experiment with future CSS properties that aren't yet full-fledged standards. It allows the browser to test and debug these new properties while the specification is being worked out.

Table 2.1 shows the current existing prefixes at the time of this writing (see http://reference.sitepoint.com/css/vendorspecific).

Table 2.1 Vendor-Specific Extensions

Prefix	Organization
`-ms-`	Microsoft
`mso-`	Microsoft Office
`-moz-`	Mozilla Foundation (Gecko-based browsers)
`-o-`	Opera Software
`-atsc-`	Advanced Television Standards Committee
`-wap-`	The WAP Forum
`-webkit-`	Safari (and other WebKit-based browsers)
`-khtml-`	Konqueror Browser

So the exciting thing here is that `border-radius` is one of the properties that browser vendors have been experimenting with for some time.

Currently, the Mozilla and WebKit family of browsers (e.g., Firefox and Safari) have implemented decent support for `border-radius` using vendor-specific prefixes. Huzzah! And we can use these properties right now. Today. Let's take a look at how they work.

Progressive Enrichment with -webkit-border-radius and -moz-border-radius

If we treat rounded corners as a visual reward to browsers that can handle them with CSS, rather than a design requirement in every possible viewing environment, we can progressively enrich our Web pages by using vendor-specific versions of `border-radius` without waiting for the CSS3 spec to reach Candidate Recommendation status.

Here's how you apply rounded corners today, using the vendor-specific extensions for Safari and Firefox (and other Mozilla- and WebKit-based browsers). The markup remains clean as a whistle, with simply a container to apply the styles to:

```
<div class="box">
  <img src="boat.jpg" alt="boat" />
</div>
```

And here's the CSS to make this box round on all four corners in Firefox and Safari:

```
.box {
  padding: 15px;
  background: #e2e1d4;
  -webkit-border-radius: 8px;
  -moz-border-radius: 8px;
  }
```

With these two rules in place, you'll be good to go in Mozilla- and WebKit-based browsers, in this case giving each corner an 8-pixel rounded radius — regardless of the width of the box. In other words, by using *CSS* to round the corners, you ensure the box will be *truly* flexible in all directions, without ever having to worry about images or color lock-in.

There's a caveat here. CSS validators (that validate against the CSS2.1 spec) will choke on the border-radius property since it's a part of spec that's not finished yet. Style sheets that contain these future properties will flag the file as invalid. Now that's okay (if you're fine with an intentionally invalid style sheet), or you may want to quarantine these forward-thinking properties to their own style sheet, which we'll talk about in just a bit.

FUTURE-PROOFING

You can go a step further and add the actual CSS3 property for browsers that might recognize it in the future:

```
.box {
  padding: 15px;
  background: #e2e1d4;
  border-radius: 8px;
  -webkit-border-radius: 8px;
  -moz-border-radius: 8px;
}
```

Out of the three rules added to the declaration, the browser will pick up the property that it recognizes and harmlessly ignore the others.

ROUNDING SPECIFIC CORNERS

So far, we've been rounding all four corners of the box with one rule, but we can also round specific corners individually by using the syntax that follows.

To round just the top-left corner (**Figure 2.7**):

```
.box {
  padding: 15px;
  background: #e2e1d4;
  border-top-left-radius: 8px;
  -webkit-border-top-left-radius: 8px;
  -moz-border-radius-topleft: 8px;
}
```

Figure 2.7

Notice that the -moz- version differs slightly from the CSS3 and -webkit- property, in that topleft is one word and comes last in the chain.

Similarly, you can specify the other three corners individually using the same syntax.

To round just the top-right corner (**Figure 2.8**):

```
border-top-right-radius: 8px;
-webkit-border-top-right-radius: 8px;
-moz-border-radius-topright: 8px;
```

Figure 2.8

To round just the bottom-left corner (**Figure 2.9**):

```
border-bottom-left-radius: 8px;
-webkit-border-bottom-left-radius: 8px;
-moz-border-radius-bottomleft: 8px;
```

To round just the bottom-right corner (**Figure 2.10**):

```
border-bottom-right-radius: 8px;
-webkit-border-bottom-right-radius: 8px;
-moz-border-radius-bottomright: 8px;
```

Combinations of any or all of these work as well—for example, rounding both the top-left and bottom-right corners (**Figure 2.11**):

```
.box {
  padding: 15px;
  background: #e2e1d4;
  border-top-left-radius: 8px;
  border-bottom-right-radius: 8px;
  -webkit-border-top-left-radius: 8px;
  -webkit-border-bottom-right-radius: 8px;
  -moz-border-radius-topleft: 8px;
  -moz-border-radius-bottomright: 8px;
}
```

All in all, it's a *very* simple set of rules that takes the headache and maintenance out of rounding corners, keeping the markup lean and mean and leveraging the power of CSS to handle the heavy lifting.

A Little Choppy in Firefox 2

It's important to point out that Firefox 2's implementation of `-moz-border-radius` was a little choppy. The corners are badly aliased. We have to cut the browser some slack, however, as it was an early implementation and experimentation. And thankfully, Firefox 3 cleaned everything up and renders things on a par with Safari.

Figure 2.12 shows a comparison of Firefox 2, Firefox 3 and Safari, all rendering the same element with rounded corners. I've darkened up the background color to #333 to heighten the contrast, so you can really see the difference between renderings.

Figure 2.9

Figure 2.10

Figure 2.11

Notice how aliased and blocky the corner looks in Firefox 2? When there's a large enough contrast between the rounded element and the background color it's sitting on, this becomes especially apparent and disappointing. Something to keep in mind.

Safari   Firefox 2   Firefox 3

Figure 2.12 Comparison of border-radius being rendered in Safari and Firefox 2 and 3.

Luckily in Firefox 3, things are fixed completely, smoothing out the way it renders the radius (**Figure 2.13**).

Figure 2.13 A zoomed view, comparing border-radius rendering in Firefox 2 and 3.

PERFECTLY FINE IF CONTRAST IS LOW

You can easily get by in Firefox 2, however, provided the contrast is low enough. Our rounded boxes on the Tugboat template, for example, are rather low contrast, and if we do the same zoomed-in comparison, you'll notice that even Firefox 2 looks good (see **Figure 2.14**). That's excellent news! While Firefox 2 was released about 3 years ago (as of the time of this writing), it still has decent support for low-contrast rounded corners.

Safari   Firefox 2   Firefox 3

Figure 2.14 Showing how Firefox 2's choppy rendering is OK if contrast is low enough.

Background Clipping

You can also combine background *images* with background colors and border-radius. Layered background images will be properly clipped and rounded as well, enabling you to create some neat effects.

For example, at the end of the "Coffee News" portion of the Tugboat template is a button to access the news archives (**Figure 2.15**). While we could pretty easily create an image to handle things, why not take advantage of border-radius plus a background image to create a flexible, editable hyperlink instead?

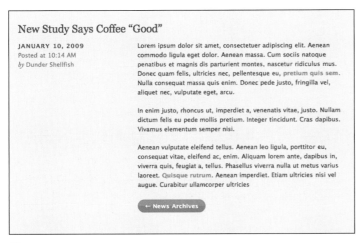

Figure 2.15

A SIMPLE HYPERLINK

The button has a "glass" effect (**Figure 2.16**), which we can achieve with a horizontally repeating semitransparent PNG that is craftily positioned. Using `border-radius` to round the ends of the button and clipping the repeating image will complete the treatment on what is essentially just a hyperlink. The markup is as simple as this:

```
<div class="more-btn"><a href="/archives/">&larr; News
Archives</a></div>
```

We've wrapped an `<a>` element in a `<div>` with a class of `more-btn`. You'll also notice that we're using the HTML entity for a left arrow, by inserting `&larr;` before the link text.

NOTE

The <div> isn't necessary, but is an appropriate block-level wrapper for a hyperlink on its own line.

Figure 2.16 A zoomed view of the button, where you can see the glass effect created by an overlayed, semitransparent PNG.

CREATING THE PNG background IMAGE

Our next step is to create the repeating PNG image that'll create the glossy effect on top of the blue background color. Follow these steps:

Create a new file in Photoshop that's 50 pixels wide by 100 pixels tall.

Fill a new layer with white.

Double the size of the canvas by adding 100 pixels to the bottom.

Reduce the opacity of the white layer to around 10%.

Save the image as a PNG-24 (you may see an option for PNG-8, but this doesn't support alpha transparency).

You're left with **Figure 2.17,** a 200-pixel-tall image with the top half white at 10 percent opacity and the bottom half completely transparent.

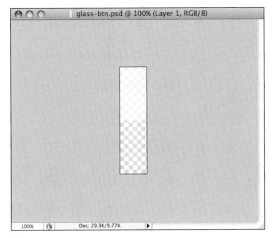

Figure 2.17

The dimensions are arbitrary here, as long as the image is much larger than you anticipate needing. That'll allow for breathing room should the text or padding around the link shrink or grow. It also means we could reuse this image on other varying-sized buttons throughout the site. Typically, I'll make tiling background images at least 2px wide (or tall) to account for smooth tiling across browsers, which at times don't like to tile images that are 1px wide (or tall).

APPLYING THE STYLES THAT CREATE THE BUTTON

Now we're ready to apply the CSS that turns these ingredients into a glossy, rounded, pill-shaped button.

First, let's add some padding and the blue background and change the link color to white (**Figure 2.18**).

```
div.more-btn a {
  padding: 5px 14px;
  color: #fff;
  background: #3792b3;
  }
```

Figure 2.18

Next, let's add the semitransparent PNG that we created earlier, tiling it horizontally (repeat-x) and positioning it vertically centered (0 50%).

```
div.more-btn a {
  padding: 5px 14px;
  color: #fff;
  background: #3792b3 url(img/glass-btn.png) repeat-x 0 50%;
}
```

Figure 2.19

Figure 2.19 shows the glass-btn.png image tiling over the blue background. Because the bottom half of the image is completely transparent, and we're centering it vertically, we get the semitransparent portion of the PNG showing on the top half of the button only, thereby creating that neat reflective look that's the rage with all the kids these days.

Now we'll add the border-radius properties that will round the button in Mozilla- and WebKit-based browsers, as well as any future supporters of the border-radius property, just as we have previously discussed in this chapter (**Figure 2.20**).

```
div.more-btn a {
  padding: 5px 14px;
  color: #fff;
  background: #3792b3 url(img/glass-btn.png) repeat-x 0 50%;
  border-radius: 14px;
  -webkit-border-radius: 14px;
  -moz-border-radius: 14px;
}
```

Figure 2.20

EASY HOVER STATES

Adding a hover treatment to the button is as easy as adding a little declaration that simply swaps out the background-color with a new value. We'll keep the link's text color and the glass-btn.png in place, but switch to a red when moused over (**Figure 2.21**).

Figure 2.21

```
div.more-btn a:hover {
  background-color: #a14141;
}
```

You can start to see the real power and flexibility of building buttons and other interactive, rounded elements this way. We can swap color, size, type treatment, and hover states, all with a few lines of code—in seconds.

ADDING A *border* DETAIL

For an extra bit of detail, we could also add a subtle border around the button, using the same color as the background. That will set the glass PNG off the edges a bit, adding a little depth to the entire button.

```
div.more-btn a {
  padding: 5px 14px;
  color: #fff;
  border: 1px solid #3792b3;
  background: #3792b3 url(img/glass-btn.png) repeat-x 0 50%;
  border-radius: 14px;
  -webkit-border-radius: 14px;
  -moz-border-radius: 14px;
}
```

Figure 2.22 shows a zoomed-in detail of that single-pixel border. It's extremely subtle, but a worthy effect to mention. Try experimenting with thicker border widths as well.

And that reminds me: While `border-radius` will round off any element's background (including color and images), it'll also round an element's `border` as well, just like it's happening here.

1px border

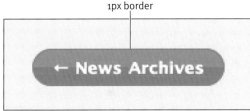

For example, let's take the same button we've been working with, but take away the background color and PNG image (replacing it with white). We'll thicken a 5px border and round that off a bit.

Figure 2.22 A zoomed view of the button, where the 1px border to offset the glassy PNG is more visible.

```
div.more-btn a {
  padding: 5px 14px;
  border: 5px solid #e2e1d4;
  background: #fff;
  border-radius: 5px;
  -webkit-border-radius: 5px;
  -moz-border-radius: 5px;
}
```

Figure 2.23 shows the results, which demonstrates `border-radius` rounding the border we've set with CSS instead of the background we'd previously used.

Figure 2.23

Figure 2.24 A zoomed view of the button in Firefox 2, which doesn't properly support background image clipping.

NO BACKGROUND CLIPPING IN FIREFOX 2

It's important to note that unfortunately background images aren't properly clipped in Firefox 2. This isn't a problem with our button currently, as the semitransparent PNG we're using will blend in on top of the tan background. If we darken the page background, however, you'll notice the background image isn't clipped by -moz-border-radius in Firefox 2 (**Figure 2.24**). You also can't help but notice the horribly aliased corners, which may have looked hip back in say, 1983. That's something to keep in mind: Again, Firefox 2's implementation of border-radius works best at low contrast, while Firefox 3's implementation is correct.

Rounding Form Elements

While we've applied border-radius to a <div> and <a> elements so far, you can apply the property to just about anything—including form elements. With a combination of background color, borders, a small tiled background image, and border-radius, you can easily create some elegantly styled form inputs that are flexible and easy to maintain.

Let's walk though a quick example of a simple comment form that we'll add to the Tugboat template.

SIMPLE FORM MARKUP

First we'll start with a basic form, including inputs for Name and Email and a <textarea> box for comments.

```
<form id="comment-form" action="/">
  <fieldset>
    <label for="name">Name</label>
    <input id="name" type="text" />
  </fieldset>
  <fieldset>
    <label for="email">Email</label>
    <input id="email" type="text" />
  </fieldset>
  <fieldset>
    <label for="comment">Comment</label>
    <textarea id="comment"></textarea>
  </fieldset>
</form>
```

We'll use the `<fieldset>` element to wrap each section of the form that includes the label and inputs.

Figure 2.25 shows the form (unstyled at this point) added to the Tugboat template.

Figure 2.25

Now we can apply a little CSS to start styling things.

APPLYING BASIC STYLES

First, let's give a bottom margin to each `<fieldset>` to space each row out a bit. Let's also apply `display: block;` to the `<label>`s, as they are inline elements by default. That'll put each label and form element on its own line. While we're at it, let's also add a small margin to the bottom of each `<label>` and make them bold as well (**Figure 2.26**).

Figure 2.26

```
#comment-form fieldset {
  margin: 0 0 15px 0;
  }
#comment-form fieldset label {
  display: block;
  margin: 0 0 3px 0;
  font-weight: bold;
  }
```

ADDING BACKGROUNDS AND REMOVING BORDERS

Next, let's create a combined declaration to style the `<input>`s and the `<textarea>` in one shot. Let's give them a width (I've arbitrarily chosen 400px in this case), add some padding, increase the font size, remove default borders, and give them a slightly darker tan background than the page (**Figure 2.27**).

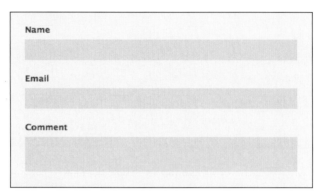

Figure 2.27

```
#comment-form fieldset input,
#comment-form fieldset textarea {
  width: 400px;
  padding: 5px;
  font-size: 1.4em;
  border: none;
  background: #e2e1d7;
  }
```

CREATING DEPTH

Let's now add back in some depth by creating a small shadow GIF that we can tile horizontally along the top of the form elements.

Figure 2.28 shows the GIF image, just a few pixels tall, that fades from a darker tan color to the background color of the form element.

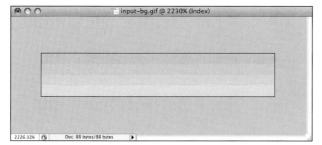

Figure 2.28

We'll add this image to the declaration that's setting styles for the `<input>`s and `<textarea>`, tiling it horizontally along the top.

```
#comment-form fieldset input,
#comment-form fieldset textarea {
  width: 400px;
  padding: 5px;
  font-size: 1.4em;
  border: none;
  background: #e2e1d7 url(../img/input-bg.gif) repeat-x top
left;
  }
```

Figure 2.29 shows the form, now with added depth thanks to our tiled gradient. The form is starting to look good, and we can make it even better with borders and `border-radius`.

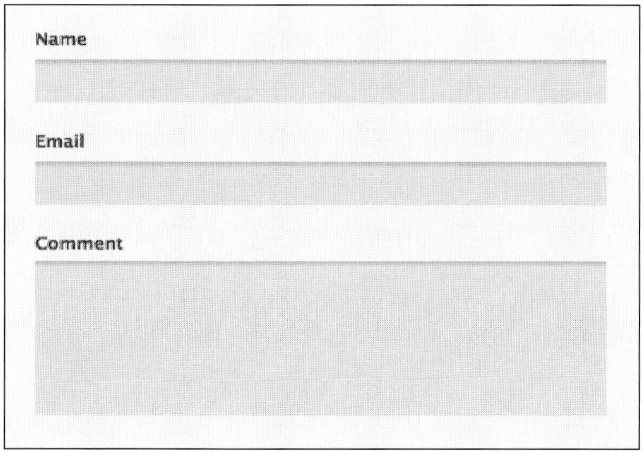

Name

Email

Comment

Figure 2.29

ADDING FURTHER DETAIL WITH
borders AND border-radius

For an extra level of added detail, we can add a 1-pixel white border on the bottom and right edges of the form elements, enhancing the idea that light is coming from the top left and creating the shadow on the inset fields (**Figure 2.30**).

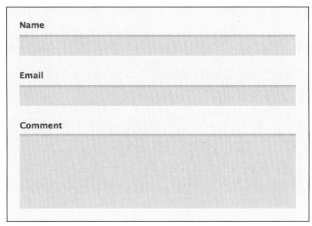

Figure 2.30

```
#comment-form fieldset input,
#comment-form fieldset textarea {
  width: 400px;
  padding: 5px;
  font-size: 1.4em;
  border: none;
  border-bottom: 1px solid #fff;
  border-right: 1px solid #fff;
  background: #e2e1d7
url(../img/input-bg.gif) repeat-x top left;
  }
```

Finally, let's add the border-radius properties that we used earlier in the chapter, rounding the corners of the <input>s and <textarea> in Mozilla- and WebKit-based browsers.

```
#comment-form fieldset input,
#comment-form fieldset textarea {
  width: 400px;
```

```
  padding: 5px;
  font-size: 1.4em;
  border: none;
  border-bottom: 1px solid #fff;
  border-right: 1px solid #fff;
  background: #e2e1d7
url(../img/input-bg.gif) repeat-x top left;
  border-radius: 5px;
  -webkit-border-radius: 5px;
  -moz-border-radius: 5px;
  }
```

Figure 2.31 shows the completed form (as viewed in Safari), where you'll notice the background and border highlights being clipped and rounded, creating a nifty three-dimensional treatment for the form elements.

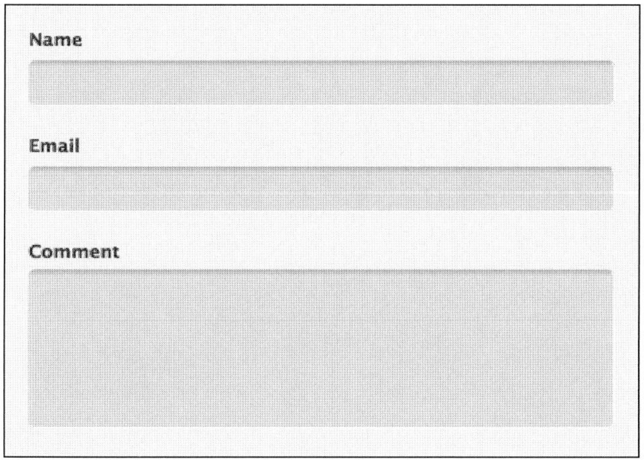

Figure 2.31

DECLARING A `:focus` STYLE

Going a step further, let's add an overriding style when the user clicks in one of the form fields. Here's a quick declaration that uses the `:focus` pseudo-element that turns both `<input>` and `<textarea>` fields' background white (**Figure 2.32**).

```
#comment-form fieldset input:focus,
#comment-form fieldset textarea:focus {
  background: #fff;
  }
```

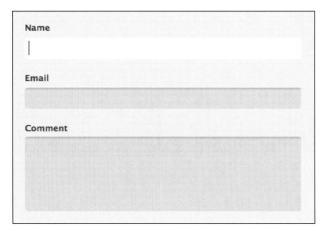

Figure 2.32

We're only overriding the background color and image here, while the rest of the styles (including the rounded corners) are inherited from our previous declaration.

What About Other Browsers?

I know what you're saying by now: "Dan, this is all well and good—but what about other browsers?"

We know that currently `border-radius` is supported in Mozilla- and WebKit-based browsers, by way of those magical vendor-specific properties (`-moz-` and `-webkit-`). And by including the CSS3 `border-radius` property along with those as we have throughout the chapter, we can ensure that any *future* browsers that choose to implement it will be supported as well.

But the elephant in the room at this point is Internet Explorer, which has no support at the time of this writing for CSS3 properties or vendor-specific extensions to CSS3 properties. What that means is that Internet Explorer will render a *square* box, button, or form element.

Let's take a look at what we've created throughout the chapter, and how things will render in browsers that don't support `border-radius`.

Figure 2.33 shows the Tugboat template viewed in IE7, where you'll notice the absence of rounded corners completely. Since IE7 doesn't understand `border-radius`, it safely ignores those properties and just renders a square box. Everything else remains the same.

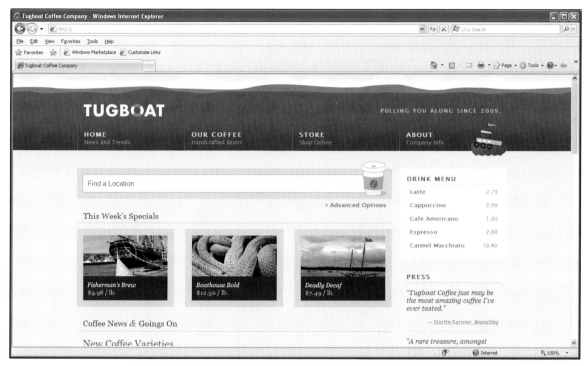

Figure 2.33 The Tugboat template as viewed in IE7 on Windows XP.

THIS IS OKAY

I realize it might *not* be okay for your client or boss—but the important thing to remember here is that this method *degrades beautifully*. Boxes and padding and positioning all remain exactly the same. The design is intact. It's functional and readable. The only difference is that elements that are rounded in more forward-thinking browsers are square here.

SQUARE BUTTON

How does our button example look in IE7? **Figure 2.34** shows a perfectly fine, albeit square, button. We still have the same padding, text, and glossy background image and color. It's functional and proportionally the same. Again, this is okay.

Figure 2.34 The button as rendered in IE7 (or any other browser that doesn't support border-radius).

SQUARE FORM ELEMENTS

And how about our rounded form `<input>`s and `<textarea>`? Well, they're square as well—but again degrade beautifully with the shadow background image and color and highlighted borders remaining intact (see **Figure 2.35**). It's a fine-looking form, even when non-rounded, don't you think?

One last time, say it with me: *This is okay.*

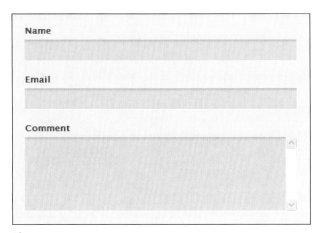

Figure 2.35

PROGRESSIVE ENRICHMENT

NOTE

I'll make much more of a case for progressive enrichment later in Chapter 4, where I'll do my best to convince you (and your clients and bosses) of the benefits of pushing the envelope a bit.

For some, the fact that your design will look slightly different, depending on which browser renders it, is not an easy thing to come to terms with. But by giving visual rewards to the browsers that *can* handle these advanced CSS properties, you're creating flexible, easily maintained designs that push the development of these new standards *forward*.

Wonderful for Prototyping

I'll wrap up this chapter by leaving you with an important point: Regardless of whether you're able to use `border-radius` in *production*, it's important (and fun) to experiment with these progressive methods. Not only are they the way forward, but they're also wonderful tools for prototyping.

Often, I lean on an iterative process when creating designs for the Web. I might start from markup and CSS-based wireframes, slowly add more detail in code, or bring later screen shots of that code into Photoshop for further tweaking.

Using border-radius during the initial design phase is a powerful tool in prototyping. The ability to quickly add a few rules that control color and/or the amount of roundness (that can later be customized) is indispensable. This facilitates a rapid, nondestructive evolution of a design. It's much easier to change a few lines of code to alter the rounded corners of a template than to redraw them in an image editor, cut them out, and reapply them as background images repeatedly. There have even been times where I've used border-radius to prototype rounded corners in the browser, only to later create images from screen shots of the rendered template.

So if there's one takeaway from this chapter I hope you'll savor, it's that border-radius (and other CSS3 properties) is no longer a pipe dream but a valuable tool that we can start using in development and production. And once you start implementing rounded corners with CSS3 as we have in this chapter, you'll never go back to the old ways.

Next up, we'll take a look at another method of progressively enriching your designs: using RGBA (red green blue alpha) color.

3

Flexible Color with RGBA

Using simpler forms and straightforward, easy-to-use instruments and controls allows you to achieve a very high level of craftsmanship. We then use color and texture to create a personality for each vehicle.

—Larry Erickson, former designer for Ford Motor Company

I once had a client (I'll call him "Stanley") who relayed the following bit of wonderful feedback after receiving a concept I'd designed for his website: "I absolutely hate the green in this design," he told me. "It reminds me of the same green in my ex-girlfriend's quilt. We can't use that green."

Stanley, a self-described nondesigner, was certainly passionate about color—or at least this one particular hue. And it's no secret that *color is emotional*. Everyone has a favorite and/or an aversion to another. There's no question that color is important and powerful, and not to mention a free, abundant resource in the world of Web design.

Larry Erickson, a former auto designer for Ford, hints at some of that power in the opening quote. That color and texture alone can be enough to create separate personalities when applied to a well-crafted structure. While he's talking about different car models, I'm sure you'll agree this applies to design in general.

In the spirit of reevaluating past methods and best practices, it's especially exciting to talk about color in regard to *alpha transparency* and the flexibility and texture that comes along with it (see **Figure 3.1**).

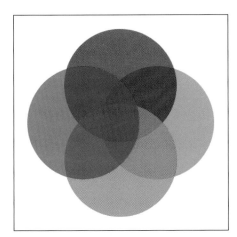

Figure 3.1 Example of semitransparent colors, layered on top of each other.

What we're talking about in terms of alpha transparency is the ability for color to have varying levels of *opacity*. This additional characteristic is yet another way that distinct personality can come from something as simple as color. The layering of semitransparent colors opens up a whole new realm of visual uniqueness that's especially engaging when used in Web interfaces.

Historically, we'd often achieve this goal by using PNG images (which can be semitransparent) or perhaps the `opacity` property (a CSS3 property that has had decent support in Firefox 1.5 and later, Safari 1.2 and later, and Opera 9 and later).

Today, an exciting new unit added to the CSS3 Color Module also provides a way of specifying a color plus a level of opacity: RGBA. RGBA offers unique advantages that we'll explore in this chapter. We'll revisit the pros and cons of the other methods mentioned as well. As we go along, we'll progressively enrich the Tugboat template using RGBA, as well as tackle the construction of the "This Week's Specials" section of images and descriptions (**Figure 3.2**). But first, an explanation of how RGBA works.

Figure 3.2

What Is RGBA?

First, let's talk about what RGB is. RGB (which stands for Red, Green, Blue) is a color model that allows you to specify color using three numerical values for each shade. You can combine them to create a multitude of hues.

Figure 3.3 shows the color picker in Photoshop, where you'll notice the blue we've chosen can be noted in a variety of ways, including the familiar hex value, which we could specify in CSS:

```
body {
  background: #3792b3;
  }
```

We could specify this same color in RGB like so, using the three numerical values for Red, Green, and Blue:

```
body {
  background: rgb(55,146,179);
  }
```

Both methods achieve the same blue using different syntax.

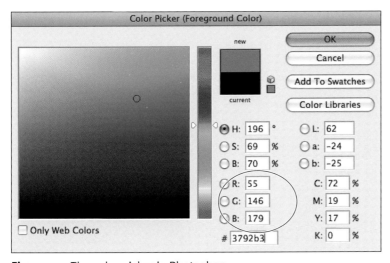

Figure 3.3 The color picker in Photoshop.

RGBA stands for Red Green Blue Alpha. The W3C explains that "The RGB color model is extended in this specification to include 'alpha' to allow specification of the opacity of a color" (http://www.w3.org/TR/css3-color/#rgba-color).

What that means is that a fourth value between 1 and 0 can be added to specify the level of opacity for the RGB color named. A value of 1 means fully opaque, while a value of 0 means fully transparent.

For example, we could specify our blue at 50% opacity by adding .5 as the fourth value after the RGB values:

```
body {
  background: rgba(55,146,179,.5);
  }
```

Figure 3.4

Figure 3.4 shows how the same shade of blue can be used with varying levels of opacity when specified with RGBA. The code to achieve that looks like the following, with the RGBA portion highlighted (and forgive me for using inline styles here for the sake of easily showing everything all at once):

```
<div style="float: left; width: 50px; height: 50px;
background: rgba(55,146,179,1);"></div>
<div style="float: left; width: 50px; height: 50px;
background: rgba(55,146,179,.75);"></div>
<div style="float: left; width: 50px; height: 50px;
background: rgba(55,146,179,.5);"></div>
<div style="float: left; width: 50px; height: 50px;
background: rgba(55,146,179,.25);"></div>
<div style="float: left; width: 50px; height: 50px;
background: rgba(55,146,179,.1);"></div>
```

You'll notice that by using the same RGB value, we can achieve differing levels of opacity: 1 is 100% opacity, .75 is the same blue at 75% opacity, .5 is 50%, and so on.

Being able to adjust the opacity of a color quickly and easily directly in the style sheet is an excellent thing. But what about the opacity property itself, and how does it differ from RGBA?

The opacity Property vs. RGBA

You can also enable transparency via CSS3 with the opacity property. Simply specify a value between 1 and 0 to determine the amount of transparency for any element.

For example, if we want to set the opacity of all paragraphs on the page to 65%, we could write this:

```
p {
  opacity: .65;
  }
```

NOTE

To learn more about opacity versus RGBA, see http://www.css3.info/ introduction-opacity-rgba/.

The big difference between opacity and RGBA is that opacity affects the transparency of the element, *and anything contained within it*, while RGBA affects the transparency of the *background or color of an element only*.

WHERE opacity GOES WRONG

For instance, let's say we have a semitransparent box of text with a blue
background that we want to layer over a patterned background (**Figure 3.5**).

Figure 3.5

The markup for this little module might look something like this:

```
<div class="coupon">
  <p>Save 50% off all coffee, this week only!</p>
</div>
```

The base styles to get the box looking right without worrying about transparency would look something like this:

```
.coupon {
  padding: 1em;
  background: #3792b3;
  border-radius: 1em;
  -webkit-border-radius: 1em;
  -moz-border-radius: 1em;
  }
.coupon p {
  font-family: Helvetica, sans-serif;
  font-size: 2em;
  font-weight: bold;
  color: #a14141;
  }
```

Notice we're putting our rounded corners to use here with the
border-radius properties from Chapter 2. Good for us.

Using the `opacity` property

If we were to use the `opacity` property here to achieve the transparency on the box, we'd need to add the rule to the `.coupon` declaration that generates the blue box.

```
.coupon {
  padding: 1em;
  background: #3792b3;
  border-radius: 1em;
  -webkit-border-radius: 1em;
  -moz-border-radius: 1em;
  opacity: .25;
  }
```

Figure 3.6 shows the results, where you can see that not only is the blue box at 25% opacity, but because the text is inside the box, it too is at 25% opacity. And that's not what we want to happen.

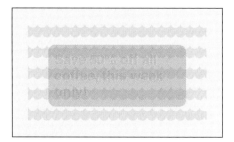

Figure 3.6

Using the RGBA color model

Rather than using the `opacity` property, let's use RGBA to specify the background color and amount of transparency of the box all in one single rule:

```
.coupon {
  padding: 1em;
  background: rgba(55,146,179,.25);
  border-radius: 1em;
  -webkit-border-radius: 1em;
  -moz-border-radius: 1em;
  opacity: .25;
  }
```

We've just swapped the background color that was previously a hex value (#3792b3) with its RGB equivalent (55,146,179). Then, by specifying the alpha value of .25, we're adjusting the opacity of that blue to 25%.

The big difference here is that by using RGBA, we're altering the transparency of the background color only, and not the entire box and its contents as the opacity property would. **Figure 3.7** shows the successful results.

Figure 3.7

Compatibility

Like the border-radius property discussed in the previous chapter, RGBA is a wonderfully flexible tool, but since it's unsupported in Internet Explorer, it's clearly a *progressive enrichment* candidate. Current support for RGBA is in WebKit (Safari, Chrome, iPhone, etc.), Firefox 3, and Opera 10. As long as you come to terms with the fact that it will only work in forward-thinking browsers, everything will be okay.

RGBA

WebKit (Safari)	✓
Firefox 3	✓
Opera 10	✓

Support for the opacity property is similar, although it was generally adopted a bit earlier than RGBA. Again, Internet Explorer offers no support.

The opacity Property

WebKit (Safari 1.2+)	✓
Firefox 1.5+	✓
Opera 9+	✓

See http://dev.opera.com/articles/view/css-and-opacity-methods-for-creating-tr/ for more info.

What About Other Browsers?

Using RGBA provides a refreshingly flexible way of adjusting a color's transparency with a simple line of code. There's a theme you'll recall from Chapter 2 as well: The ability to manage design details from the style sheet rather than editing images not only makes your life easier, but also frees you up to work faster and more efficiently—the browser assumes all the heavy lifting. Again, this is the future direction of CSS, and we can start experimenting with that now in the browsers that support advanced styles such as RGBA.

Fortunately, using the RGBA color model syntax is harmless for browsers that don't yet support it. For example, Internet Explorer will just ignore the rule altogether.

PROVIDING A BACKUP FOR CHALLENGED BROWSERS

Since browsers like Internet Explorer ignore a rule where RGBA is involved, we must specify a backup color prior to declaring the RGBA one.

For instance, if in our example we want to add an alternate, solid hue of light blue for browsers that don't support RGBA, we can do so by ordering things like this:

```
.coupon {
  padding: 1em;
  background: #c4dada; /* for IE */
  background: rgba(55,146,179,.25); /* for browsers that
➥support RGBA */
  border-radius: 1em;
  -webkit-border-radius: 1em;
  -moz-border-radius: 1em;
}
```

Figure 3.8 shows how things might look in Internet Explorer or another browser that doesn't support RGBA (or border-radius). We've specified a solid light blue as an alternative, first in the declaration and then overriding that solid color with an RGBA value at 25% opacity for browsers that do support it. This is progressive enrichment at its finest!

Granted, you'll lose the transparency in browsers that don't support RGBA, but you'll still be in control of the colors completely within the style sheet. Fancy transparency for forward-thinking browsers—and a solid alternative that's functional and readable for others.

Figure 3.8 How the example might look in browsers that don't support RGBA or `border-radius`.

USING TILED PNGS

Another option (which would work in more browsers) is a tiled PNG. The PNG format supports an alpha channel, and therefore can be used as a background image to create a semitransparent box as we've done using RGBA.

For example, if we create a small PNG image by filling in a layer with our blue at 25% opacity (**Figure 3.9**), we can then set that as a tiled background image on the box to achieve the same effect.

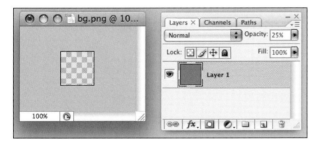

Figure 3.9 Creating a "tileable" semitransparent PNG in Photoshop.

```
.coupon {
  padding: 1em;
  background: url(../img/bg.png);
  border-radius: 1em;
  -webkit-border-radius: 1em;
  -moz-border-radius: 1em;
}
```

PNGs with alpha transparency work in Safari, Firefox, and Opera just as RGBA does, but also in Internet Explorer versions 7 and 8. Version 6 supports PNG images but doesn't support the alpha channel, so your semitransparent PNGs will be completely opaque when viewed in IE6.

There are various hacks to get PNG alpha channel support working in IE6, some that involve using JavaScript and some that include using Microsoft's proprietary `filter` CSS property (if the PNG is being called as a background image).

Tied to a color palette and level of opacity

Again, as with using images for rounded corners, using tiled PNGs to set semitransparent backgrounds has its downside: You're tied to a particular color and amount of transparency when dealing with images. If you use RGBA to handle these situations, you can adjust hue and level of opacity in seconds right in the style sheet—no carving out of new images when a new color or adjustment to transparency is needed. The importance of this detail will certainly be a consideration to factor in when you're deciding which method you choose—but if it's okay to have a solid color or other alternative for browsers that don't yet support RGBA, then by all means start experimenting.

An Excellent Tool for Prototyping

I made the same argument in Chapter 2 when we were talking about using `border-radius`, and the same applies here when discussing RGBA. Regardless of whether or not you use RGBA in production, it can still be a valuable tool when prototyping interfaces. That is, if you are using Safari, Firefox, or even Opera to initially develop your designs in, then RGBA is a wonderful way of iterating with color and transparency. Changes and adjustments are made quickly and painlessly in code. Once you're happy, you can choose the appropriate method for the final implementation, whether that's RGBA and a backup for other browsers, or perhaps a PNG image that works as well in IE7+.

So again, a big takeaway from this chapter is that it's not too early to experiment with RGBA. You can even use it in production if you're on board with the concept of progressive enrichment.

Not Just for Backgrounds

Another unique advantage of RGBA is that it's not just for backgrounds. You could also use RGBA to specify the color and transparency of *hypertext*. This opens up another host of possibilities and elegant but flexible solutions.

For example, I've used RGBA to lower the opacity of a portion of a hyperlink on my studio's site, http://simplebits.com.

BLENDING TEXT WITH RGBA

Figure 3.10 shows a small list of links, each with a bold heading and normal-weight subheading. I could choose a root color green for the links, while plugging that same green into an RGBA value with slightly decreased opacity to desaturate things a bit.

Figure 3.10

In other words, instead of choosing two colors for the link, I can choose just one and let RGBA lighten the color, blending it into the background a bit to create a desaturated alternative.

These links are marked up as an unordered list, with the <a> element surrounding the icon, title (wrapped in <strong>), and subheading:

```
<ul class="lst group">
  <li>
    <a href="http://iconshoppe.com/">
      <img src="/img/ishoppe-25.gif" alt="icon" />
      <strong>IconShoppe</strong> Icons to go.
    </a>
  </li>
  <li>
    <a href="http://foamee.com/">
      <img src="/img/foamee-25.gif" alt="icon" />
      <strong>Foamee</strong> Who do you owe?
    </a>
  </li>
</ul>
```

The CSS that handles the link color would look like this:

```
ul.lst li a {
  color: #76a65c; /* for all browsers */
  color: rgba(118,166,92,.75); /* for browsers that support
⮑RGBA */
  }
ul.lst li a strong {
  display: block;
  color: #76a65c; /* override for browsers that support RGBA */
  }
```

Figure 3.11 Showing one solid link color in browsers that don't support RGBA.

As you can see, we're specifying an RGBA value at 75% for the entire link, then overriding that with the same exact color green at 100% (using the hex equivalent) on the `<strong>` element. We've also added `display: block;` to put the title on its own line.

This method takes some of the guesswork out of choosing different shades of the same color. You need only choose one root color, then use RGBA to create varying opacities of the same color.

Browsers that don't yet support RGBA will ignore the *rgba* rule, and instead just use the root color that we specified with `color: #76a65c;` (**Figure 3.11**).

WILSONMINER.COM

Wilson Miner uses RGBA in a similar fashion on his website (**Figure 3.12**), where he reduces the opacity of black text in order to blend it into the colored background (check it out at http://wilsonminer.com).

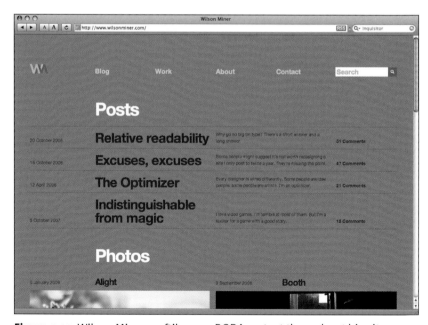

Figure 3.12 Wilson Miner craftily uses RGBA on text throughout his site.

He explains in a blog post (http://www.wilsonminer.com/posts/2008/oct/15/excuses-excuses/):

> *I wanted to branch out this time, but I wanted some flexibility, so I built the site frame and homepage to adapt to different colors and backgrounds. I started with the classic green, but that will change periodically.*
>
> *The homepage in particular uses RGBA color values to add transparency to the text so it picks up the background tone, whether it's a solid color or an image. Even the "black" text on the homepage is slightly transparent, which gives it just a hint of the background color. It softens the contrast a bit, and it reminds me of the effect when I used to overprint colors in print design.*

So, while a majority of the text on Wilson's site is black, he uses RGBA to knock that down a bit and blend that same black into whatever the background color happens to be (**Figure 3.13**). He can change the background color while keeping the text color and varying opacity levels the same. The semitransparent text will always pick up tones from the background color behind it. Now that's flexible color.

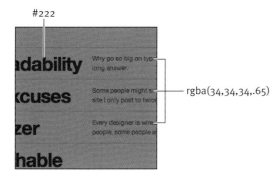

Figure 3.13

EASY HOVER SELECTION

Another clever use of RGBA is to make it easy to choose a hover color for link text. By simply reducing the opacity of a link's color, you have an instant hover treatment for links—no need to choose a second color. And the flexibility is there should you ever change the background color of the page or base link color.

I've implemented this on the Tugboat template, where the hover color is just a semitransparent version of the original link color (**Figure 3.14**).

```
a:link, a:visited {
  font-weight: bold;
  text-decoration: none;
  outline: none;
  color: #3792b3;
  }
a:hover {
  color: rgba(55,146,179,.65);
  }
```

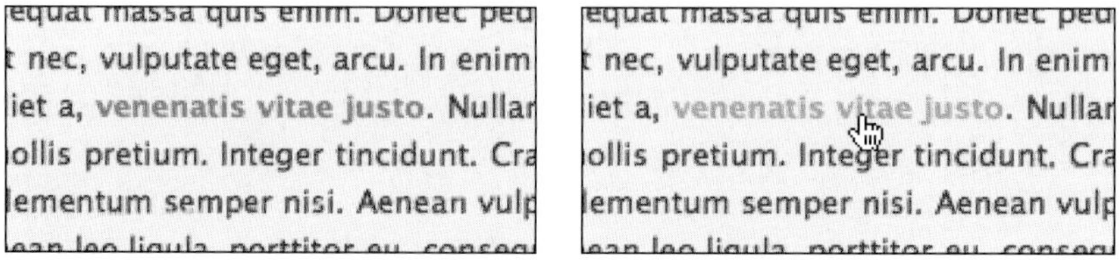

Figure 3.14 Showing normal and hovered link text (zoomed).

PAINTING BY NUMBERS

This color blending reminds me of a fascinating interview with Art Lozzi, a former background painter for Hanna-Barbera back in the 1960s. John Kricfalusi (creator of the infamous cartoon series *Ren & Stimpy*) highlights Art's work (see **Figure 3.15** for a sample) in a blog post, analyzing the backgrounds he painted for the Yogi Bear cartoon (read the full interview here: http://johnkstuff.blogspot.com/2006/12/color-theory-art-lozzi-explains-some.html).

Lozzi, referring to the way they painted the overall background color first:

> *This color is rolled on (onto the thickish Bristol paper we used, not board and not canvas) and everything was painted on top of it so that if there were any "holes" or spaces, the sky color would tie it all together.*

Figure 3.15 One of Art Lozzi's beautiful background paintings.

In response, Kricfalusi then offers this insight regarding Art Lozzi's technique:

> You can see the peach sky in the little holes in the hills where the sponge didn't paint. This gives the effect of mixing the main BG color with the other colors in the BG and it ties them all into one harmonious color scheme.

> You can also see the hill color behind and through the tress and so forth.

> Blending the colors makes all the objects in the BG part of a family of color, rather than having a bunch of separate objects each with completely different colors splitting up the image and all competing for attention.

Blending color to create a harmonious palette. Something Art was doing decades ago with *paint and brushes*, and exactly what Wilson Miner was doing when he used RGBA to blend a single text color into the background color on the Web. Craftsmanship spans mediums!

Constructing "This Week's Specials"

Figure 3.16

Now that we have a good handle on what RGBA is and how it works, as well as other means of creating transparency on the Web, let's circle back to the Tugboat template and dissect the "This Week's Specials" section. Next, we'll walk through the implementation, using RGBA to create the screen overlays on each photo (**Figure 3.16**).

Each photo has a title and price that sits on top of a semitransparent overlay. This is a common design pattern on the Web, a flexible way of adding meta-information to photos that may contain a variety of photos underneath, each with different shades/color/contrast. To ensure legibility of the text, a semi-transparent background is used so that it works no matter what photo is behind it. A perfect place to play with RGBA.

CRAFTING THE MARKUP

Let's begin with the markup. We'll use an unordered list to structure the three specials, and inside each list item, we want the entire image, the title, and the price to be clickable. Therefore, we'll wrap everything in <a> elements, resorting to inline elements within to call out the title and price (since block-level elements can't live inside a hyperlink).

There are a few extra elements added here as well, and the necessity for those will become clear as we build the styles to make the finished product.

```
<ol class="specials">
  <li>
    <div class="special">
      <div class="special-img">
        <a href="/specials/fb">
          <img src="img/boat.jpg" alt="ship" />
          <span>
            <strong>Fisherman&#8217;s Brew</strong>
            <em>$9.98 / lb.</em>
          </span>
        </a>
      </div>
    </div>
  </li>
  <li>
    <div class="special">
```

```
      <div class="special-img">
        <a href="/specials/bb">
          <img src="img/ropes.jpg" alt="ropes" />
          <span>
            <strong>Boathouse Bold</strong>
            <em>$12.50 / lb.</em>
          </span>
        </a>
      </div>
    </div>
  </li>
  <li>
    <div class="special">
      <div class="special-img">
        <a href="/specials/dd">
          <img src="img/fame.jpg" alt="sailboat" />
          <span>
            <strong>Deadly Decaf</strong>
            <em>$7.49 / lb.</em>
          </span>
        </a>
      </div>
    </div>
  </li>
</ol>
```

MAKING THE LIST HORIZONTAL

Our first few rules for the style sheet involve setting a width for each list item, and floating each to the left in order to turn the list from vertical to horizontal.

```
ol.specials li {
  width: 210px;
  float: left;
  margin: 0 15px 1.5em 0;
  }
```

Figure 3.17 shows the results of adding that first declaration, where we see each image linked along with the title and price below. Each image is 210 pixels wide, and we've added some margins on the right and bottom of each item.

NOTE

Remember, as mentioned back in the Introduction, we're applying these styles based on the fact that we're also applying a reset.css style sheet to zero out the normal browser defaults.

Figure 3.17

ADDING THE ROUNDED BORDER

Taking what we learned from Chapter 2, let's add a 15-pixel border to each item, rounding it using the border-radius properties we now know and love. We'll also increase the width of each list item by 30 pixels to account for that new border.

```
ol.specials li {
   width: 240px;
   float: left;
   margin: 0 15px 1.5em 0;
   }
ol.specials li div.special {
   position: relative;
   border: 15px solid #e2e1d4;
   border-radius: 8px;
   -webkit-border-radius: 8px;
   -moz-border-radius: 8px;
   }
```

We've added position: relative; to each list item as well, paving the way for positioning the title and price on top of each photo. **Figure 3.18** shows the rounded border added, and we're now ready to start positioning the overlay.

Figure 3.18

POSITIONING THE OVERLAY

Next, let's position the title and price overlay. While we want the entire image to be clickable, we'll utilize the `<span>` that surrounds the title and price, making it a block-level element and positioning that on top, anchored to the bottom of the photo.

The following declaration takes care of a whole host of things, including positioning and setting the base font styles for the title and price. For now, we've also set a dark gray background for the overlay.

```
ol.specials li div.special a span {
  display: block;
  position: absolute;
  width: 100%;
  bottom: 0;
  left: 0;
  font-family: Georgia, serif;
  font-size: 1.1em;
  font-weight: normal;
  line-height: 1.3em;
  color: #ccc;
  background: #333;
  }
```

Figure 3.19 shows the progress thus far. You'll notice we need some padding and additional typography tweaks applied to the title and price to get things looking as they should.

Figure 3.19

STYLING THE TITLE AND PRICE

Now we'll adjust the typography and spacing of the title and price, creating two new declarations that give 10 pixels of padding around the text, change the color, as well as set `display: block;` since both `<strong>` and `<em>` are inline elements by default. That'll put both title and price on their own separate lines.

```
ol.specials li div.special a span strong {
  display: block;
  padding: 10px 10px 0 10px;
  font-weight: normal;
  font-style: italic;
  color: #fff;
  }
ol.specials li div.special a span em {
  display: block;
  padding: 0 10px 10px 10px;
  font-style: normal;
  color: #e3c887;
  }
```

Figure 3.20 shows those two declarations being applied, and we're almost done!

Figure 3.20

ADDING RGBA TO THE OVERLAY

Our final step is to add an RGBA value to make the overlay's background transparent—in this case, black at 70% opacity.

```
ol.specials li div.special a span {
  display: block;
  position: absolute;
  width: 100%;
  bottom: 0;
  left: 0;
```

```
font-family: Georgia, serif;
font-size: 1.1em;
font-weight: normal;
line-height: 1.3em;
color: #ccc;
background: #333;
background: rgba(0,0,0,.7);
}
```

We'll keep the previous #333 value for browsers that don't yet understand RGBA, keeping the text readable no matter what photo lies behind it. But we'll override that with our RGBA value, black at 70% opacity. **Figure 3.21** shows the finished list, where we have a nice flexible style for the overlay of each special.

Figure 3.21

Quick, easy alterations

Adjusting the color and level of opacity on the overlay is as easy as updating one CSS rule. For example, if we want to make the overlay red, we can quickly and easily do that by modifying the RGB value (**Figure 3.22**).

```
ol.specials li div.special a span {
  display: block;
  position: absolute;
  width: 100%;
  bottom: 0;
  left: 0;
  font-family: Georgia, serif;
  font-size: 1.1em;
  font-weight: normal;
  line-height: 1.3em;
  color: #ccc;
```

(continued on next page)

```
background: #600;
background: rgba(102,0,0,.7);
}
```

Figure 3.22

Wrapping Up

We've just scratched the surface of what is possible with RGBA. But I hope the examples shown in the chapter have ignited a spark and you'll experiment with adding transparency to your designs. The ability to specify opacity along with color is a flexible, powerful tool—and RGBA is just one of the many ways to achieve that. It does so quickly and easily, and that's why we like it. Like border-radius, its browser support is limited at present, but with WebKit, Mozilla, and Opera browsers leading the way, it's a technique that you can experiment with and use today, whether it's for prototyping and iterating, or pushing the envelope in production on public-facing projects.

After two straight chapters covering CSS3 properties and advanced techniques that don't render the same in every browser, it's time to stop and gain some perspective. Do websites need to look exactly the same in every browser? In the next chapter, we'll discuss just that, along with some more progressive enrichment fun.

4

Do Websites Need to Look Exactly the Same in Every Browser?

I've always thought of myself as an 80 percenter. I like to throw myself passionately into a sport or activity until I reach about an 80 percent proficiency level. To go beyond that requires an obsession and degree of specialization that doesn't appeal to me.

—Yvon Chouinard, *Let My People Go Surfing*,
founder and owner, Patagonia, Inc.

Ever try talking to (or working with) someone who is 100% obsessed with a single task? The danger is that they'll get bogged down in details. *Every* detail. On the other hand, an "80 percenter," as Patagonia founder Yvon Chouinard defines it, might eventually learn to know which details to focus on. Determining *which* details are the most important and beneficial can be just as useful as knowing them all.

Like Yvon, I'd also call myself an 80 percenter. It doesn't mean I'm lazy; it means I acknowledge the possibility of being obsessive about details that might not matter as much to others.

If we apply this thinking to Web design, it's easy to become obsessive about details. Years ago, I used to pride myself in being able to implement designs down to the pixel-level across every browser I could get my hands on. I wasn't alone, of course. Back in the days of nested tables and spacer GIF shims, accessibility, findability, flexibility, and other -ibilities didn't matter. What mattered was that a design rendered *exactly the same*—no matter what.

We've come a long way since then. And so have browsers. The speed in which browsers are adopting standards has increased rapidly. We've spent the last two chapters talking about CSS3 goodies that some browsers are already implementing—before the spec is even finished. This accelerated adoption is exciting, and arms us designers with more tools to work with and techniques to make our lives easier. However, not every browser is on the same track, and therefore we need to be careful about what we pick and choose to utilize.

But most important, is a shift in thinking: It's okay if a design looks slightly different in one browser than it does in another. Once the designer and decision makers accept this, and *embrace* it, it's then that the concept of progressive enrichment can be fully leveraged.

So. Do websites need to look exactly the same in every browser? Let's find out.

The Answer I'm Sticking to

When I registered the domain dowebsitesneedtolookexactlythesameinevery browser.com, I set out to design the appropriate answer in a simple, straightforward manner (**Figure 4.1**). While somewhat humorous, this simplistic site actually renders differently, depending on the browser you're viewing it in (more on that in a bit).

Figure 4.1

Now that we've answered the question this chapter's title asks, I think we can move on.

No? If only it were that simple.

Rewarding vs. "This Is Broken"

Previously, we talked about adding rounded corners and alpha-transparent color using forward-thinking CSS3—neither of which work in Internet Explorer. Let's compare the Tugboat template as viewed in Safari on the Mac (**Figure 4.2**) versus Internet Explorer 8 in Windows (**Figure 4.3**).

Figure 4.2

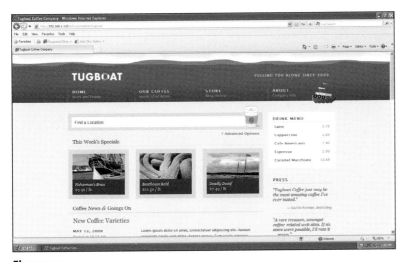

Figure 4.3

Layout, color, typography, and proportions between the two browsers are almost identical. However, where the corners are rounded in Safari, they're square in Internet Explorer 8 (IE8). The semitransparent screen overlaying the photos in Safari is solid black in IE8. These details aren't crucial to the design, readability, and functionality of the Tugboat site, so the variation is perfectly okay in this case.

We should treat these visual details as *rewards* for the browsers that support the advanced code that creates them, rather than something *missing* or *broken* in the browsers that don't yet support that advanced code. That's a big shift in thinking for a lot of folks: that the design isn't broken in IE8... that we weren't lazy in not visually aligning every possible browser. We're visually rewarding users of browsers that are forward thinking, while allowing other browsers to degrade in a perfectly acceptable fashion. That's the core of what I'm talking about when using the term *progressive enrichment*.

Decision Makers Who Get It

Accepting that a design might look slightly different depending on the browser isn't going to sit well with everyone. And if the decision maker of the group isn't on board, it makes the idea of progressive enrichment a tough sell. But that doesn't mean we shouldn't talk about it.

For example, convincing decision makers that it's far more flexible and efficient to implement rounded corners with CSS3 might be a tough road, depending on the team involved.

Take for instance, Twitter (http://twitter.com), a popular social messaging application that allows people to send short status updates via the Web or text messages.

If you compare my own Twitter homepage in two recent browsers, you'll notice the top navigation and main content container are rounded in Safari (**Figure 4.4**), while those same page elements are square boxes in IE8 (**Figure 4.5**).

Twitter is using the `border-radius` properties we discussed in Chapter 2 to handle the rounding here, and the decision makers are okay with things looking slightly different between browsers.

Figure 4.4 Twitter viewed in Safari, where `-webkit-border-radius` rounds the corners of various page elements.

Figure 4.5 Twitter viewed in IE8, where the absence of rounded corners degrades perfectly fine to square boxes around the top navigation and main content area.

It makes good sense to use CSS3 to handle the rounded corners in Twitter's case, as the background color and the image (a screenshot of the classic video game Pitfall, in my case) as well as the background color of the sidebar are all customizable by the user. Using CSS3 to round the corners made this flexibility possible without the use of extra markup or scripting. *Speed* and *bandwidth* are of the essence for Twitter, and the rounded corners in Mozilla- and WebKit-based browsers are visual rewards rather than necessary requirements.

All of this is okay since the absence of rounded corners doesn't hinder the layout, readability, and functionality of the site.

EASIER WHEN *YOU* ARE THE DECISION MAKER

All of these forward-thinking solutions are far easier when it's *you* who is the decision maker. In other words, for your own projects, or if you happen to be lucky enough to be the one calling the shots when it comes to design implementation, the concept of progressive enrichment becomes more and more like an attractive path. And addictive.

For example, I created a ridiculously useless site called Foamee (http://foamee.com), which suggested syntax for sending beer and coffee IOUs via Twitter (**Figure 4.6**). The title of each page has decorative ornaments that sit flush against the text on the left and right of the text.

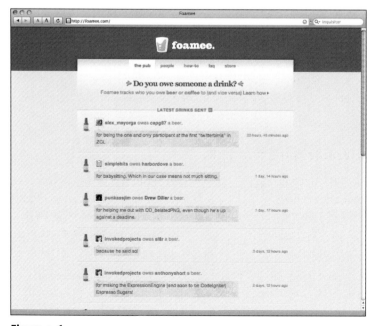

Figure 4.6

Now, I could've added extraneous markup, and used some CSS trickery to center align the text, yet keep the ornaments snug against either side of the text no matter its length (something that really should be simple to implement yet isn't cross-browser)—but instead I chose to use *generated content* with CSS to simplify things drastically while maintaining flexibility.

I could keep the markup extra simple, using just an `<h1>` element:

```
<h1>simplebits</h1>
```

And I could use the `:before` and `:after` pseudo-elements to insert the ornament images just to the left and just to the right of the text:

```
h1:before {
  content: url(../img/ornament-left.gif);
  }
h1:after {
  content: url(../img/ornament-right.gif);
  }
```

Figure 4.7 shows how this will look in browsers that support the `:before` and `:after` pseudo-elements, with the ornament images properly sitting snugly around the `<h1>`. IE6 and 7 *don't* support generated content, however, and thus ignore those declarations entirely. This is likely why we haven't seen widespread use of these handy CSS solutions.

Figure 4.7

Figure 4.8 shows how they would display the title, where the ornaments don't appear (as in IE6 or IE7). This is okay! And since *I* was the decision maker here, it was an easy trade-off. The title is still there, it's readable and styled the same, and the absence of the ornaments is the only differing issue. And I've managed to keep the markup and styles simple, flexible, and bulletproof.

Figure 4.8

Golf clap for Internet Explorer 8

The additional good news here, is that IE8 *does* support the `:before` and `:after` pseudo-elements, further supporting the use of these CSS solutions going forward. If you can live with IE6 and IE7 looking slightly different, then it might be time to reevaluate the use of these previously unsupported selectors from here on.

This is part of the "reevaluating of past methods" I referred to in the Introduction. We've grown accustomed to avoiding certain CSS selectors and properties because they weren't supported in whatever the current crop of browsers was at the time. It's always a good idea to check now and again if that support has changed.

For example, `:before` and `:after` pseudo-selectors have long been unsupported in Internet Explorer, but since that's no longer true with IE8, we can take that into consideration when choosing solutions. Is your current problem better handled with a few simple CSS rules for the latest browsers, letting older versions of IE show less ornamentation? Most of the time, I'd likely answer, "yes."

Not only accepting, but *embracing* browser deficiencies

Designer and author Andy Clarke takes a drastic and somewhat humorous approach in visually distinguishing IE6 from other browsers. **Figure 4.9** shows his beautiful website viewed in both Safari (on the left) and IE6 (on the right). Andy is serving an alternate black-and-white version of his website to IE6 users, encouraging them to upgrade in order to get the full-color experience.

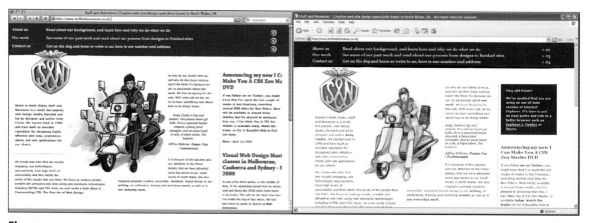

Figure 4.9

This not only answers the question "Do websites need to look exactly the same in every browser?" but it also embraces that difference intentionally. Would this work for every situation? No. But there *is* something that can help you decide how far to take things: *statistics*.

It All Comes Down to Stats

What's the most important factor when you're deciding whether to use CSS that's not supported in all browsers? Statistics, naturally. You could ask questions like, "When can we use CSS3 to round corners? When can we rely on RGBA to handle alpha-transparent color? When is it safe to stop worrying about how things look in IE6?" But everything depends on the particular site you're working on.

Eric Meyer, someone who knows a thing or two about CSS, left a comment on my blog over five years ago (http://simplebits.com/notebook/2004/12/17/ie5.html#comment53) in response to the question, "When can we hide CSS from IE/Mac?" It's still stuck with me today, and it can be applied to any browser-support question.

> *The answer is simple: when* your *site's (or sites' if you have more than one) user logs tell you that you can. Not before then. The user stats from other sites, or from global-aggregation surveys, are worse than useless.*

Here's what Eric was saying: It doesn't matter what the *global* statistics for a particular browser are; what matters most are the statistics for the site you happen to be working on.

Are most of your visitors still using IE6? Well then, you might think twice about using extensive progressive enrichment techniques. However, if IE6 visitors are a measly 1%, then by all means push the envelope.

Statistics for *your* site might be an aid in trying to make a case for advanced styles to the decision makers you are working with. Or those statistics may have the opposite effect.

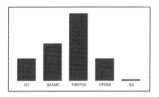

Figure 4.10 If your stats look like this, push the envelope!

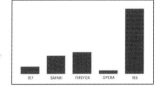

Figure 4.11 If your stats look like this, you'll probably want to use progressive enrichment sparingly (after openly weeping, of course).

More Advanced CSS That Works Today

Now that we've attempted to make the case for websites not having to look the same in every browser, let's explore a few more advanced CSS and vendor-specific CSS3 properties that we can experiment with to further progressively enrich the Tugboat template.

TEXT-SHADOW

Safari 1+	✓
Firefox 3.5	✓
Konqueror	✓
iCab	✓
Opera 9.5+	✓

Originally introduced in CSS2, the `text-shadow` property allows shadow effects to be applied to text. Safari was the first and only browser to implement `text-shadow` way back in Version 1. But it's now also currently supported in Opera 9.5, Konqueror, and iCab, and was also added to Firefox 3.5 (see http://www.css3.info/preview/text-shadow/).

I used `text-shadow` to treat the "*No!*" text on the dowebsitesneedtolook exactlythesameineverybrowser.com site that I mentioned earlier (**Figure 4.12**). The simplistic site practices what it preaches, while viewers in IE or older versions of Firefox, for example, will see unshadowed text.

Figure 4.12 A zoomed view of the text with `text-shadow` applied in Safari.

Let's walk through another example. We'll begin by adding a drop shadow to the navigation text of the Tugboat template. The navigation is marked up as an unordered list, and we'll add the `text-shadow` property to each link.

```
#nav ul li a {
  text-shadow: 2px 2px 4px #000;
  }
```

The syntax here is essentially saying, "Offset the shadow 2 pixels to the right of the text and 2 pixels down from the bottom of the text" (negative values can be used to go in the opposite direction). The third value is assigning an optional 4px blur to the shadow, and the last piece assigns a color for the shadow.

Figure 4.13 shows the results as viewed in Safari, where you'll notice the drop shadow added to the navigation text. By adjusting the four values in the rule (horizontal offset, vertical offset, blur amount, and color), a variety of effects can be achieved.

Figure 4.13

Using RGBA in combination with text-shadow

We used straight black (#000) for the shadow color earlier, but what if we want to soften it up a bit and use what we learned in Chapter 3? Choosing a slightly darker brown than the background color is one option, but even simpler, and more flexible, is to use an RGBA value. We could use black again, but let's ratchet down the opacity a bit so that it blends with the brown background.

```
#nav ul li a {
   text-shadow: 2px 2px 4px rgba(0,0,0,.7);
   }
```

So instead of solid black, we're specifying black at 70% opacity using RGBA. **Figure 4.14** shows the same shadow we applied initially, but now with a more subtle dark brown created by blending black on brown.

Figure 4.14

NOTE

Just remember, once again, that using these properties will likely prevent your style sheet from validating against the CSS 2.1 spec. You may want to quarantine these rules into their own style sheet if you're obsessive about seeing that green success message, or alternatively, just be okay with your main style sheet being invalid (which I believe to be perfectly fine). Fear not the *intentional* validation error.

NOTE

Just a reminder that RGBA doesn't work in all browsers yet. Refer back to Chapter 3 for details.

Using RGBA here took the guesswork out of choosing a shadow color that would work well with the brown background, and we have the added flexibility of being able to change the background color without changing the shadow.

Bevel effects with text-shadow and RGBA

Sometimes, the `text-shadow` property is used to create a bevel effect on text. With a tight shadow that highlights the background color ever so slightly, it's a great candidate for RGBA.

If we use a negative value to pull the shadow above the text by 1 pixel, and then use a slightly transparent black with *no* blur, it creates the illusion that the text is sunken into the brown background with a light source directly above the text (**Figure 4.15**).

Figure 4.15 A zoomed view of the nav text with `text-shadow` used to create a bevel effect.

```
#nav ul li a {
  text-shadow: 0 -1px 0 rgba(0,0,0,.8);
  }
```

Alternatively, we could use a lighter color *below* the text for similar effects. Take the button example from Chapter 2, for instance, where we can adjust the colors as well as add a 1px, nonblurred text shadow of white at 80% opacity.

```
div.more-btn a {
  padding: 6px 14px;
  text-shadow: 0 1px 0 rgba(255,255,255,.8);
  color: #777;
  border: 1px solid #ccc;
  background: #ccc url(img/glass-btn.png) repeat-x 0 50%;
  border-radius: 14px;
  -webkit-border-radius: 14px;
  -moz-border-radius: 14px;
  }
```

Figure 4.16 shows the results, with the button taking on a Mac OS-esque appearance, due to its new highlight around the *bottom* of the text.

Figure 4.16 A zoomed view of the button with `text-shadow` creating an inset look for the text.

Again, `text-shadow` has limited browser support at present, but can act as a visual reward to those that do support it. It also degrades quite nicely, since it's merely an effect attached to what should be readable hypertext.

BOX-SHADOW

Similar to the `text-shadow` property, `box-shadow` allows a shadow effect to be applied to any *element*. The syntax is essentially the same, with horizontal and vertical offsets followed by blur amount and color value.

Creating truly flexible drop shadows using images and CSS is often an annoying chore, while having to allot space in a layout grid for a fixed-width shadow. Multiple images are also required to create shadows that resize along with the container they're applied to. However, by putting the burden of a drop shadow on CSS, they can be an afterthought, adjustable at any time.

Current support for `box-shadow` certainly isn't wonderful, but with Firefox 3.5 coming on board, I'm sure we'll start to see a lot more sites using it to handle drop shadows, just as we're starting to see rounded corners handled more and more through CSS3.

Safari 1+	✓
Firefox 3.5	✓

Applying box-shadow to Tugboat

For example, let's apply a subtle shadow on each of the "This Week's Specials" boxes on the Tugboat template.

If you'll recall from Chapter 3, the "Specials" boxes are structured in an ordered list, with a `<div class="special">` containing the image and metadata for each item. This `<div>` has the `border-radius` rules that we learned about in Chapter 2 attached to it as well (**Figure 4.17**).

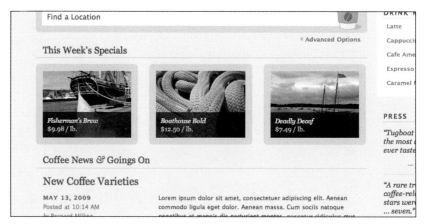

Figure 4.17

```
ol.specials li div.special {
  border: 15px solid #e2e1d4;
  background: #e2e1d4;
  border-radius: 8px;
  -webkit-border-radius: 8px;
  -moz-border-radius: 8px;
}
```

We'll add the box-shadow properties to this declaration in the same way we did with border-radius back in Chapter 2—by adding the vendor-specific properties for Safari (-webkit-box-shadow, which is currently supported) and Firefox (-moz-box-shadow, which will be supported in the upcoming version 3.1) as well as the official CSS3 box-shadow property itself for any browser that eventually chooses to support it.

```
ol.specials li div.special {
  border: 15px solid #e2e1d4;
  background: #e2e1d4;
  border-radius: 8px;
  -webkit-border-radius: 8px;
  -moz-border-radius: 8px;
  box-shadow: 2px 2px 4px #bdbcb0;
  -webkit-box-shadow: 2px 2px 4px #bdbcb0;
  -moz-box-shadow: 2px 2px 4px #bdbcb0;
}
```

We've just specified a shadow 2 pixels to the right, 2 pixels from the top, a blur of 4 pixels, and a darker tan than the border color. **Figure 4.18** shows the results, where you'll notice that when used in combination with `border-radius` (which was already in place on each box), the shadow also recognizes that curved border and correctly draws the shadow behind it (**Figure 4.19**).

Figure 4.18

Figure 4.19 A zoomed view of one of the rounded corners, showing the shadow properly following the curve.

So, in just a few lines of code, we've created an editable, flexible shadowed, rounded box entirely using CSS3. Now, remember, not all browsers support `box-shadow` (hello, Internet Explorer) and the user won't see a shadow (or rounded corner) in those browsers. But again, at the risk of sounding like a broken record, that's perfectly okay if you're all right with square, unshadowed boxes for a portion of your visitors.

Using RGBA in combination with box-shadow

Just as we did with `text-shadow`, the color value we specify here for the `box-shadow` could also be an RGBA value, where the opacity could be adjusted to blend the hue into the background color (for browsers that support RGBA, that is).

Instead of the dark tan we previously had chosen (#bdbcb0), let's just use straight black, at a reduced opacity to create a reusable shadow that will blend into any background color using RGBA.

```
ol.specials li div.special {
  border: 15px solid #e2e1d4;
  background: #e2e1d4;
  border-radius: 8px;
  -webkit-border-radius: 8px;
  -moz-border-radius: 8px;
  box-shadow: 2px 2px 4px rgba(0,0,0,.3);
  -webkit-box-shadow: 2px 2px 4px rgba(0,0,0,.3);
  -moz-box-shadow: 2px 2px 4px rgba(0,0,0,.3);
}
```

Figure 4.20

The results are very similar (**Figure 4.20**) to choosing a hex color that's darker than the background, but by using black at 30% opacity, it means if the background color changes—to, say, red, blue, or green—the box-shadow/RGBA combo will just continue to work without any adjustments (**Figure 4.21**), since it's still black at 30% opacity overlaying whatever the background happens to be.

Figure 4.21

Since Safari and Firefox are the only two browsers supporting box-shadow at the time of this writing and they both support RGBA, using RGBA for the shadow color here seems like a perfectly fine thing to do. Back in Chapter 3, we specified *backup* hex colors for browsers that didn't yet support RGBA, but here we can avoid it.

-WEBKIT-TRANSITION

File this one under "eye-candy that elicits ooohs and aaahs." WebKit has been experimenting with CSS animation: A perfectly wonderful candidate for progressive enrichment, the -webkit-transition property allows for some pretty *flashy* stuff, all done with plain ol' CSS. Now, these whiz-bang tricks will *only* work in Safari currently—but the absence of these animation effects is harmless, and hardly missed by the browsers that don't support them.

And here is where I wish I could embed video into the pages of this book, because we're talking about a visual effect here, and writing about it just doesn't do it justice. But I'll do my best.

Be sure to check out this Surfin' Safari blog post (http://webkit.org/blog/138/css-animation/) on the subject of CSS animation, where some of the amazing possibilities were demonstrated back in October 2007 (**Figure 4.22**).

Figure 4.22

Spin and rotate HTML elements, fade things in/out on hovering or clicking, ease in/out border widths and padding—there are some previously unheard of effects that can all be had with a few simple rules of (vendor-specific) CSS.

Adding hover fades to Tugboat

As an example of how simple it can be to add subtle-but-effective treatments to say, the navigation links of a website, let's use the `-webkit-transition` property to fade in and out the background that's shown when nav items are hovered over. This little example merely scratches the surface as to what's possible with CSS transitions, but it should be enough to get you started.

The navigation for Tugboat (**Figure 4.23**) is housed in an unordered list wrapped with a `<div id="nav">`, with each link in a separate list item. This is a pretty typical structure for navigation these days. A simplified version of the markup would go something like this:

```
<div id="nav">
  <ul>
    <li><a href="/"><strong>Home <em>News and Trends</em>
➥</strong></a></li>
    ...
    </li>
  </ul>
</div>
```

The `<strong>` and `<em>` elements provide ways of styling the two parts of the link uniquely.

Figure 4.23

For a simple hover treatment, we could simply add a background color behind the link text. And because the header background that sits behind the navigation is a slight gradient (**Figure 4.24**), why not use RGBA here and use a slightly transparent color to let that gradient show through just a bit?

Figure 4.24 A zoomed view of the gradient that sits behind the site's navigation, going from darker brown (bottom) to slightly lighter brown (top).

```
#nav li a:hover {
  background: #000;
  background: rgba(0,0,0,.15);
  }
```

We're using black yet again to take the guesswork out of picking a darker brown than the nav is by default; we're just toning down to 15% opacity with our RGBA value. We've also specified a backup hex color for browsers that don't yet support RGBA.

Figure 4.25 shows the nav being hovered over, and because of our RGBA value at 15% opacity, the background gradient can still show through a little, making it less harsh behind the link text.

Figure 4.25

Now things get exciting when we add a -webkit-transition to the mix. If we add a transition to the background color of a certain time length, hovering over the nav items will *fade* in and out the background color when hovered over.

```
#nav li a:hover {
  background: #000;
  background: rgba(0,0,0,.15);
  }
#nav li a {
  -webkit-transition-property: background-color;
  -webkit-transition-duration: .4s;
  -webkit-transition-timing-function: linear;
  }
```

Here we've added three properties to each nav link that control the transition:

1. -webkit-transition-property assigns the property in which the transition should occur (in this case, the background color).

2. -webkit-transition-duration controls how long the transition should take (in this case, just under half a second).

3. `-webkit-transition-timing-function` controls how the speed changes over the course of the duration of the transition—in this case, `linear`, but there are other options as well that remind me of frustrating calculus homework. (Check out the complete spec by visiting http://webkit.org/specs/CSSVisualEffects/CSSTransitions.html).

Alternatively, you could use the shorthand method by combining these properties into one like so:

```
#nav li a {
  -webkit-transition: background-color;
  -webkit-transition-duration: .4s;
  -webkit-transition-timing-function: linear;
  -webkit-transition: background-color .4s linear;
}
```

The result, well, I wish I could show you here (and **Figure 4.26** is but a feeble attempt), but it's the kind of effect you'd historically see only in Flash-based elements, now happening rather easily just with CSS. It's an incredibly subtle effect—the kind of thing not everyone would notice (and more still, only Safari users will see for now). But it's incredibly simple to implement and harmless for browsers that don't understand it. Craftsmanship is the tiny, sometimes not-so-obvious details.

Figure 4.26

Applying transitions to hyperlink text color

We could also apply a transition to *all* text hyperlinks on the page, adding a similar fade-in/fade-out effect to the link's color (rather than a background as we've done previously).

By sliding in the `-webkit-transition` property to the main declaration for all links on the page, and changing the target property to `color` rather than `background-color`, we'll get a fade-in/fade-out on the hover color specified when links are hovered over.

Here are our two declarations for links *without* the transition. You'll remember from Chapter 3 that we're craftily using an RGBA value for `:hover`, using the normal link color and just reducing the opacity a bit to 65%:

```
a:link, a:visited {
  font-weight: bold;
  text-decoration: none;
  outline: none;
  color: #3792b3;
  }
a:hover {
  color: rgba(55,146,179,.65);
  }
```

Now let's add the transition rule on the normal link state. I've shortened the duration a bit here to .2s, as a bit quicker of a reaction seems to feel better on regular hyperlinks:

```
a:link, a:visited {
  font-weight: bold;
  text-decoration: none;
  outline: none;
  color: #3792b3;
  -webkit-transition: color .2s linear;
  }
a:hover {
  color: rgba(55,146,179,.65);
  }
```

The result is a subtle fade effect on hyperlinks that's sure to wow your Safari-loving friends (**Figure 4.27** is yet another feeble attempt at showing animation, and you're probably wondering why I didn't try to make a flipbook to illustrate this). Again, no fuss, no muss in other browsers, where they'll ignore the one single rule it takes to make it happen.

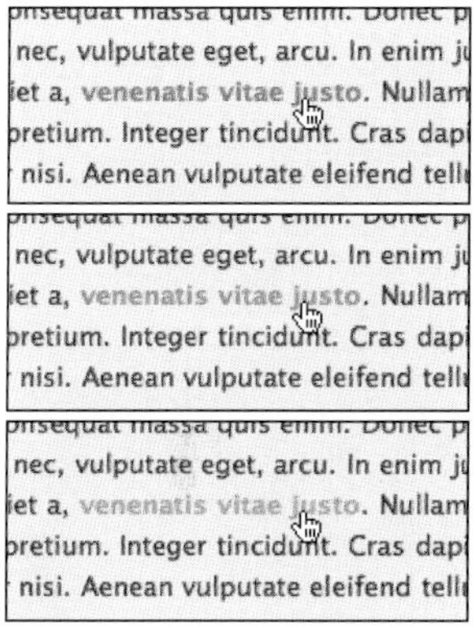

Figure 4.27

Wrapping Up

Do websites need to look exactly the same in every browser? If your answer is no, then you'll suddenly be freed up to take advantage of all the fun CSS3 stuff we've been talking about throughout the book thus far. By treating these progressive enrichments as *visual rewards*, rather than design requirements, you'll suddenly have more simplistic, flexible, easier-to-maintain options at your disposal. And the hope here is that by experimenting with these properties *now*, or even using them in production, you'll have a leg up on things as more and more browsers add support for these burgeoning standards.

Is it okay if a box is rounded in one browser and square in another? Sure, as long as the readability and functionality remains the same—and that's what's most important.

Let's try to be 80 percenters, focusing on the details that matter more than creating complex solutions to visual problems best taken care of by sensible code and browsers that have the foresight to support it.

5

Modular Float Management

The critical distinction between a craftsman and an expert is what happens after a sufficient level of expertise has been achieved. The expert will do everything she can to remain wedded to a single context, narrowing the scope of her learning, her practice, and her projects. The craftsman has the courage and humility to set aside her expertise and pick up an unfamiliar technology or learn a new domain.

—Dave Hoover, in an article on StickyMinds.com

One of the points I'm attempting to stress in the book is how important it is to *reevaluate past methods and best practices.* This is especially critical in the field of Web design, as browsers are constantly evolving, implementing new standards, and pushing ahead at an increasingly rapid pace. What was a best practice two or three years ago might be the opposite in today's browser landscape. A hack or patch to work around a certain browser in the past might not be necessary now. A CSS property that didn't have widespread support among browsers a while back might've finally reached the tipping point, opening up easier ways of accomplishing a design goal.

I'm certainly guilty of *not* reevaluating in some cases, and it's caused me to continue using workarounds for situations that are better handled by solutions that were previously thought of as "not yet ready for prime-time." I've also historically ignored pushing the envelope in using cutting-edge technologies, thinking that I'll pay close attention when things hit the mainstream.

But all of that has shifted a bit, which is hopefully coming through in these pages. Part of the reevaluation comes from *letting go*. We spent a good portion of the previous chapter talking about how it's okay if a design looks different across various browsers. That's a reevaluation in and of itself, and being okay with that variation opens up a wide range of CSS3 properties that are being implemented in forward-thinking browsers today.

Another part of the reevaluation is taking a look back at best practices, and seeing if each practice still holds true. Is there a better, easier way to handle what I'm trying to accomplish? Has this particular solution become a habit that was once harmless, but now can be improved upon?

A good craftsman will ask questions like these and reevaluate her methods if it improves the final product. Dave Hoover alludes to this in the opening quote. He compares an expert to a craftsman, heralding the courage that she might call upon to step away from the unfamiliar in order to learn new skills. A craftsman won't be afraid to reevaluate methods and best practices, and will avoid getting stuck with a narrow, singularly focused view on how to solve a particular design implementation problem.

So, in this chapter, we're going to reevaluate the concept of "self-clearing floats," which on the surface sounds dull, boring, and surely not the sort of stuff you'd think an entire chapter would be devoted to. But (sadly) floats are still the best method we have for ensuring flexibility in our layouts using CSS, and maintaining a smart, efficient way of handling them is prime reevaluation material.

Float Refresher

I'm sure by now you're all too familiar with the problems that floats can cause. Although floats offer the best option to date for handling most layout configurations with CSS, *containing* them has always been the primary cause for frustration.

Take, for example, an image inside a white box, with a <div> of text floating over to the right (**Figure 5.1**). Its simplified markup structure might look something like this:

```
<div class="box">
  <img src="/img/latte.jpg" alt="Latte at Stumptown" />
  <p class="description">Lorem ipsum dolor ...</p>
</div>
```

And its CSS might look something like this:

```
div.box {
  background: #fff;
  }
div.box img {
  width: 25%;
  }
div.box p.description {
  float: right;
  width: 70%;
  }
```

NOTE

I've intentionally left out some details here to quickly illustrate the important point. And oh, you might be wondering, "Why are we sizing an image's width with a percentage?" Just wait until the next chapter, where Ethan Marcotte shows us anything's possible.

Figure 5.1

Figure 5.2 illustrates a common problem: If the floated element (a paragraph of text in this case) is taller than the nonfloated element (the latte image), it will escape outside the container element (cue sad trombone).

Figure 5.2 When float containment goes wrong.

In a perfect world, a container would be aware of its contents, stretching to contain whatever's floated inside them. Alas, that's not how floats work. But it's through no fault of their own—floats weren't designed to do the complex (or even not-so-complex) layout configurations we use them for.

We have instead found creative ways of forcing a container to clear any floats that occur within it. And several methods are available that achieve that. I'm not going to waste pulp going over them here, as I've already done so in *Bulletproof Web Design* (New Riders, 2007).

I'll instead focus on the one solution I've come to rely on because of its robustness in clearing floats under the widest variety of circumstances.

EASY CLEARING

You might remember from Chapter 4 that :before and :after aren't supported in IE7 and below.

Initially published back in 2004 at the indispensable Position Is Everything site, *How to Clear Floats Without Structural Markup* (http://positioniseverything.net/easyclearing.html) describes a method for automatically clearing any floats that occur within a given container. The technique uses the :after pseudo-element in CSS to insert a period after the containing element, clear floats, and then hide that period from view. It's a clever solution, and one that requires additional trickery for the various versions of IE.

Now again, there are other ways to accomplish this same goal, but this is the one I've stuck by, as it's proved to be the most bulletproof.

For additional methods of self-clearing floats in a container, check out this SitePoint article, which rounds up several popular solutions: http://www.sitepoint.com/blogs/2005/02/26/simple-clearing-of-floats/.

Applying .clearfix

To illustrate how the method works, let's apply it to the previous example, where our longish paragraph of text was busting out of its box. The Easy Clearing method suggests creating a .clearfix class that contains the following rules:

```
.clearfix:after {
  content: ".";
  display: block;
  height: 0;
  clear: both;
  visibility: hidden;
  }
```

You'd apply this .clearfix class to any containing element where you'd like floats automatically cleared in. This approach will handle things nicely in browsers that support the :after pseudo-element, but not in IE. For IE versions 6 and 7, you need to apply two additional rules that effectively handle the float containment by taking advantage of their specific quirks.

ADDITIONAL RULES FOR IE6 AND 7

For IE6, you can simply create a rule that adds an arbitrary height to the container:

```
/* for IE6 */
* html .clearfix {
  height: 1%;
  }
```

And for IE7, adding a `min-height: 1px` does the trick, again using a wacky-looking selector hack to target IE7 only:

```
/* for IE7 */
*:first-child+html .group {
  min-height: 1px;
  }
```

And finally, in IE8, here's the absurd syntax we can use to target and clear floats specifically in Microsoft's latest browser:

```
* /_**(.)/*+:@//\*+html!~/rofl**/ {
  clear: please !reallyreallyimportantomg;
  }
```

Kidding! Just making sure you're paying attention.

No, in fact the good news is that IE8 supports the `:before` and `:after` pseudo-elements, so no extra declarations are needed. IE8 will recognize the initial rule that utilizes `:after`.

With those three rules in place, you have a self-clearing solution that works cross-browser.

ADDING .CLEARFIX TO THE MARKUP

Retuning to our example markup, let's now apply the `.clearfix` class to the containing `<div>` that surrounds the floated text and image:

```
<div class="box clearfix">
  <img src="/img/latte.jpg" alt="Latte at Stumptown" />
  <p class="description">Lorem ipsum dolor ...</p>
</div>
```

By adding the `.clearfix` class to the container, the three declarations we've set up will automatically clear all floats inside, ensuring this box of text and images will remain a self-contained module, independent of its surroundings.

TIP

Instead of using a selector hack to target different versions of IE, you could alternately use conditional comments to quarantine those declarations into separate style sheets for each IE version.

A Semantic Dilemma

Now here's where the reevaluation comes into play. Granted, this self-clearing technique was written over 5 years ago, so we certainly can't fault the original authors—but it's the term "clearfix" that's used here as the class name that I found particularly troubling.

The advantage to setting up these classes ahead of time is that you can attach this `.clearfix` to any element you need to contain floats in while you're developing. The problem is that, if you're like me, you're attaching this class to a lot of elements on the page. Again, floating is our best approach to flexible design, and ensuring that these floats are properly cleared is crucial in creating bulletproof interfaces. Separate portions of the page can remain independent, and you can move them around without affecting the position of other elements in the layout.

So, the downside to using a term like "clearfix" to handle this is that your templates quickly become littered with this nonsemantic term. It's confusing.

Imagine your client or boss wading through the markup seeing "clearfix" everywhere. What's so wrong that needs to be fixed all over the layout?

ONE ALTERNATIVE: A BIG LONG LIST

An alternative to using a class name is to use a single declaration that lists every element you'd like the clear fix applied to. This keeps the class out of the markup entirely, but requires you to be vigilant about maintaining the list.

For example, instead of using `.clearfix`, we'd specify each element we'd like the fix applied to by creating a combined declaration:

```
div.box:after,
#header:after,
#nav:after {
  content: ".";
  display: block;
  height: 0;
  clear: both;
  visibility: hidden;
  }
```

This works okay for small sites, with a limited number of elements on the page—but for most designs, the list can quickly become unwieldy and a chore to maintain. If you edit or delete classes in the future, that needs to be reflected in this clear fix declaration as well. And furthermore, you'll be updating it in three places: here in the `:after` declaration, as well as the two other declarations for IE6 and IE7.

A potential maintenance headache

I experienced the pain of this maintenance firsthand while working on the CSS for MTV.com (**Figure 5.3**). We'd taken the list approach to handling the auto-clearing of all the modules for the entire site—one that's complex and has many different layout configurations and floated content.

Figure 5.3 MTV.com, circa Spring 2009.

The following is a snapshot of MTV's list, where as you can see, it evolved into an absolute *beast* of page components that needed to self-clear floats. Class names were eventually changed, or removed, and remembering to update this list (and the similar lists for IE) became about as fun as alphabetizing your trash.

```
#header:after,
#memberbar:after,
#nav:after,
#wrap:after,
#wrap-inner:after,
div.main-feature:after,
div.marquee-half:after,
ol.slat li:after,
ol.promo:after,
ol.threeby:after,
ol.fourby:after,
ol.pop:after,
div.vidclips:after,
ul.vid-toggle:after,
div.full ol li:after,
div.full ol li a:after,
div.main-artist:after,
p.alpha-list:after,
div.twocol:after,
div.twocol-row:after,
div.mtv2-twocol:after,
div.threecol:after,
div.threecol ul:after,
#wrap ol.gallery:after,
.results:after,
.results-nav:after,
div.main-graphic:after,
div.flipbook-thumbs:after,
ul.rateit:after,
div.tabnav ul:after,
ol.cmnts li div.cmnt:after,
div.lyrics-wrap:after,
div.lyricsearch-main:after {
  content: ".";
  display: block;
  height: 0;
  clear: both;
  visibility: hidden;
  }
```

So, while creating a list of elements you'd like the clear fix applied to removes the need to add a class to the markup, it's a slippery slope to go down when you're dealing with an average-to-large website.

CHOOSING A BETTER CLASS NAME

So, we reevaluate. Five years ago, using a class name of `.clearfix` likely seemed harmless, but we're smarter, *craftier* now, aren't we?

Not that long ago, I began using `.group` as a class name to use for self-clearing. Semantically, I think it makes a bit more sense. We're saying that the container is a "group" of items that happens to have floats applied. "Group," to me, makes good sense.

Here it is, added to our previous example, in place of `.clearfix`:

```
<div class="box group">
  <img src="/img/latte.jpg" alt="Latte at Stumptown" />
  <p class="description">Lorem ipsum dolor ...</p>
</div>
```

Doesn't that look beautiful? Well, an improvement, anyway.

We're stretching what it means to be semantic here, I realize—but `.group` is at least *attempting* to apply meaning to the container, while `.clearfix` is just calling attention to the problem. Seeing `.group` attached to various elements in the markup shouldn't look suspicious or alarming to those who don't want (or need) to understand the complexities of laying out Web pages using floats.

Setting Up .group in Your Style Sheets

With a better class name chosen, we can now set up our clear fix declarations in order to reuse that `.group` class throughout the design, where needed. I like to quarantine my IE hacks and patches in their own style sheet (often called `ie.css`) in order to keep the clean, hack-free CSS separated.

Figure 5.4 shows the three declarations needed to set up a self-clearing fix for all browsers, with the :after trick in the main master.css file and the two patches needed for IE6 and 7 in their own ie.css file.

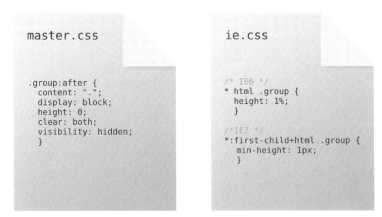

```
master.css

.group:after {
    content: ".";
    display: block;
    height: 0;
    clear: both;
    visibility: hidden;
}
```

```
ie.css

/* IE6 */
* html .group {
    height: 1%;
}

/*IE7 */
*:first-child+html .group {
    min-height: 1px;
}
```

Figure 5.4 Quarantining IE hacks and patches into their own style sheet.

You'll notice I'm using the * html and *:first-child+html selector hacks to target only IE6 and IE7, respectively, but alternatively, you could create separate style sheets for IE6 and IE7 (**Figure 5.5**) and use conditional comments in the <head> of the document to serve the appropriate fixes to the appropriate browser:

```
<head>
<link href="/css/master.css" media="screen, projection"
➥rel="stylesheet" type="text/css" />

<!--[if IE 6]>
  <link href="/css/ie6.css" media="screen, projection"
➥rel="stylesheet" type="text/css" />
<![endif]-->

<!--[if IE 7]>
  <link href="/css/ie7.css" media="screen, projection"
➥rel="stylesheet" type="text/css" />
<![endif]-->
</head>
```

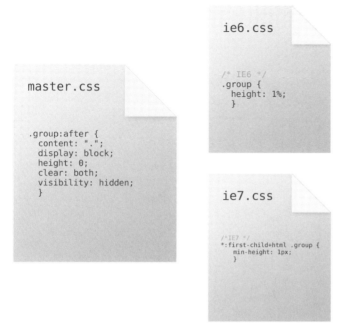

Figure 5.5 Setting up separate style sheets for the various versions of IE, to be included by conditional comments.

SET IT AND FORGET IT

The nice thing about having the clear fix set up with a semantic class name, with patches in place for all browsers, is that you now know you can apply .group to any element on the page while designing. When you're presented with a container that needs floats cleared within, just apply the .group class to that container and sleep well at night knowing that container will be independent, flexible, and able to be moved around without disturbing the rest of the layout.

It's something I rarely think about now—a trusty tool that's at my disposal. While developing a design, I know I can attach .group to an element and floats will be contained within. No worrying about maintaining lists; no littering the markup with a curious class name.

This preparation is also part of a larger setup, that of a framework of sorts, writing often-repeated code once, then reusing that in future projects. Let's talk frameworks for a moment.

Frameworks for Handcrafters

"Do you use a CSS framework?"

I'll hear that question a lot. The idea of prestructured set of style sheets and markup has caught on a bit in recent years (see **Figure 5.6** for two popular examples). Although they can be an interesting tool for learning, I prefer to create my own.

Figure 5.6 Two popular CSS frameworks: Blueprint (http://blueprintcss.org) and 960 Grid System (http://960.gs).

A CSS framework is a prebuilt set of HTML and CSS files that are generic enough to be used as a base structure for various projects. There are several popular versions out there, each with a unique focus. The idea is that you would use this prepared set of files to begin each project, where layout, typography, and all the basic code that's shared among most websites is already written for you.

I tend to recommend checking out CSS frameworks for quick-and-dirty rapid prototyping and wireframing or as a learning tool only, preferring to start from scratch for each site I'm developing. More often than not, I'd be stripping away much of the unneeded portions of the framework in order to properly support the design. In other words, you're in danger of using unnecessary cruft when using a prebuilt framework.

That said, there *are* things we can learn from frameworks. And there are certainly snippets of code that do get reused between projects I'm working on—no matter what the design becomes, visually. Identifying those commonly used pieces is helpful in *creating* a CSS framework. Your own, that is.

ROLLING YOUR OWN

So, yes. I *do* use a CSS framework—it just happens to be a very simple one that I've created myself, and I'll duplicate and reuse it at the beginning of any project (**Figure 5.7**). And I'm not alone, of course; any good craftsman does the same, often *creating* their own tools, determining the constants that appear regardless of the design—a clean slate that's ready to be added to at the start of every project.

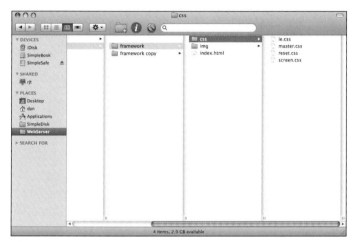

Figure 5.7 Basic file structure of the extremely simplistic bare-bones framework that I duplicate and reuse to kick off every project.

The "clear fix" setup that we've been discussing in this chapter is just a part of that framework. The declarations that handle the .group self-clearing are baked into the standard set of style sheets that I duplicate for each design (in master.css and ie.css). I wrote them once, knowing that I can count on the .group class to do its job whenever it's called upon in the markup.

Next, let's walk through my framework's style sheet structure, where I'll note the interesting bits along the way while sharing the code for each CSS file.

INDEX.HTML

First, let's talk about the HTML file that acts as the default template I'll use and duplicate for each project. I cleverly name it index.html, but you could easily come up with something craftier.

Inside index.html is a simple, bare-bones structure with "stubs" for the various elements that I anticipate using on any given project. There are a few things in particular that I'd like to point out here.

Choose a doctype, but don't sweat it

I'm using the XHTML 1.0 Transitional doctype here, and have been for several years. Will that always be the case? Probably not. While we've been focusing on the advances that CSS has been making throughout this book, things are evolving on the markup side as well. HTML 5 and XHTML 2 are both moving forward, making their case as the future of HTML on the Web. All signs are pointing to HTML 5 as being the frontrunner at this point, but only time will tell. HTML 5 is experimental at best, in today's current crop of browsers.

So for now, I'm sticking to XHTML 1.0 as it's comfortable, and I like the rules it places on the markup in terms of validation (you must use lowercase tags, elements must be closed, etc.). But it's increasingly becoming evident that whether you use HTML 4.01 Strict, XHTML 1.0 Transitional, or XHTML 1.0 Strict, for instance, doesn't make a gigantic difference to the end user.

Hiding all styles from IE6

Eight years ago, Jeffrey Zeldman wrote "To Hell with Bad Browsers" (http://www.alistapart.com/articles/tohell), signaling the dawning of "The CSS Age." Explaining how the use of @import for referencing style sheets is ignored by Netscape 4 was an important step in shedding the problems related to supporting an ancient browser. *Eight. Years.*

Completely ignoring a browser in terms of CSS is a wonderfully freeing thing. It certainly can't be done on every site. The important thing to remember is that a site's statistics should determine what level of support you decide to offer. We discussed this a bit in the previous chapter.

TIP

For what it's worth, Steve Souders has done some extensive research on how using @import to load style sheets in different configurations can affect load time and page performance. Check out his findings here: http://www.stevesouders.com/blog/2009/04/09/dont-use-import/.

Later, IE5/Mac became a problem. I began giving it the same "talk to the hand" treatment that Netscape 4 was receiving by using the backslash comment hack that I'll explain a bit more further on:

```
/* import stylesheets and hide from IE/Mac \*/
@import url("screen.css");
/* end import and hide */
```

Presently, IE6 has become the source of our frustrations—and for certain sites, giving it an unstyled, naked view is exactly what I want to do. Alpha-channel PNGs, min-width, max-width, rendering bugs galore—there are plenty of sites I've designed and maintain where the IE6 stats are low enough to drop the axe and move on. Now is the time!

So what's the easiest solution? After a bit of Googling, I found an article by Simon Clayson (http://www.simonclayson.co.uk/reportage/ie_6_text_only/), where he cleverly utilized conditional comments to hide the `<link>` element that linked to the style sheets. I blogged about this on SimpleBits (http://simplebits.com/notebook/2009/02/13/iegone.html), and from the comments emerged a simplified version that I use today in my framework as well as several live projects:

```
<!--[if gte IE 7]><!-->
<link rel="stylesheet" type="text/css" media="screen,
➡projection" href="css/screen.css" />
<!-- <![endif]-->
```

This hides all styles (assuming they're all contained within `screen.css`) from all versions of IE6 and lower, but properly serves them to all other browsers. Lucky visitors who are using IE6 or lower will get an unstyled view of the site, just like the lucky visitors using Netscape 4 have been getting for close to a decade.

Simon's original method also serves up a bare-bones CSS file specifically for IE6, but I think that's being too polite. Another real-world example of this method in practice is The Rissington Podcast (http://therissingtonpodcast. co.uk), which cleverly serves an IE6-specific style sheet complete with text rendered in Comic Sans for added rib jabbing (**Figure 5.8**).

Figure 5.8 The Rissington Podcast site, as viewed in IE6, where a mostly styleless version of the site is served, complete with text set in Comic Sans.

Regardless of whether you serve alternate styles or just hide them all, what's nice about this approach is that you're not having IE6 import all your styles, having to worry about overriding them later. You could serve IE6 with a minimal style sheet starting completely from scratch. Or none at all.

Is it a bit hacky? Sure. But in *certain situations*, not having the burden to worry about IE6 seems well worth it—and it's certainly not too early to start experimenting with methods for hiding styles from IE6 (and downright exciting to even be talking about it).

At the very least, consider this method another tool for the arsenal, when the time is appropriate.

The odd ASCII comment at the bottom

Just before the `</body>` element in my framework's default `index.html`, there sits a curious little string of four commented characters:

```
<!-- c(~) -->
```

I've gotten several e-mails about this little guy from various folks who have noticed it at the bottom of the HTML source in all (or most of) the sites I've designed. It's there because I've placed it here in the framework once, and it (along with all the other markup) serves as a base for every project I work on.

So what is it? Consider it a "maker's mark" of sorts, just like a craftsman potter etches his or her initials into the bottom of the clay pot after it's finished.

It's the ASCII equivalent of a mug of beer (handle on the left side, beer sloshing slightly inside it), and seems fitting to finish a long template of HTML code with a refreshing beverage, doesn't it?

An important detail? Certainly not. And perhaps for the purposes of this book, it'd be better if it were a mug of *coffee*, or perhaps even a coffee *bean*:

```
<!-- (ʃ) -->
```

Folks could even get more obsessive and stick entire ASCII versions of their *logo* in a commented section of a style sheet as an "easter egg" of sorts (**Figure 5.9**). I wonder who'd be crazy enough to waste all that useless code? *cough*

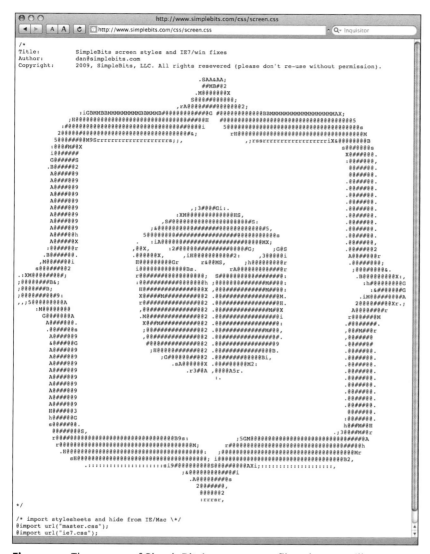

Figure 5.9 The source of SimpleBits' `screen.css` file, where you'll see a large ASCII version of the logo mark added as a comment.

Okay, and now on to more important matters! Here is the HTML file I use as a base for the CSS framework, in its entirety, for your viewing pleasure:

```
<!DOCTYPE html PUBLIC "-//W3C//DTD XHTML 1.0 Transitional//EN"
        "http://www.w3.org/TR/xhtml1/DTD/xhtml1-
➥transitional.dtd">
<html xmlns="http://www.w3.org/1999/xhtml" xml:lang="en"
➥lang="en">
```
(continued on next page)

TIP

Don't worry, I didn't spend a week carefully typing an ASCII logo out by hand, but rather used a handy little free service from Photo2Text.com (http://www.photo2text.com). Just upload an image file and the site will magically return an ASCII rendering of it. Impress your friends by claiming you took the time to create this yourself.

```html
<head>
<meta http-equiv="content-type" content="text/html;
➥charset=utf-8" />
<title>Untitled</title>
<!--[if gte IE 7]><!-->
<link rel="stylesheet" type="text/css" media="screen,
➥projection" href="css/screen.css" />
<!-- <![endif]-->
</head>

<body>

<div id="wrap">

<div id="header" class="group">
  <div id="logo">
    logo
  </div>

  <ul id="nav">
    <li><a href="#">Link</a></li>
    <li><a href="#">Link</a></li>
    <li><a href="#">Link</a></li>
    <li><a href="#">Link</a></li>
  </ul>
</div> <!-- /header -->

<hr />

<div class="group">
  <div id="main">
    main
  </div> <!-- /main -->

  <hr />

  <div id="secondary">
    secondary
  </div> <!-- /secondary -->
</div> <!-- /.group -->
```

```
<hr />

<div id="footer">
  footer
</div> <!-- /footer -->

</div> <!-- /wrap -->

<!-- c(~) -->
</body>
</html>
```

Next, let's traverse through each of the four CSS files I use that sets the structure for the styles at the start of each project.

SCREEN.CSS

This is the main style sheet that's linked to from the HTML source. Essentially, it's nothing more than a list of the other style sheets to be imported. The order in which they're imported is important, and we'll get to that in just a minute.

```
/*
Title:    Screen styles and IE/Win patches
Author:   dan@simplebits.com
*/

/* import stylesheets and hide from IE/Mac \*/
@import url("reset.css");
@import url("master.css");
@import url("ie.css");
/* end import/hide */
```

One important thing to note here is the backslash that appears at the end of this line:

```
/* import stylesheets and hide from IE/Mac \*/
```

That innocent little backslash exposes a bug that forces IE/Mac to ignore any CSS that follows it, hiding it until another CSS comment is added (hence the /* end import/hide */, in case there's ever CSS that you would want IE/Mac to understand).

IE/Mac is now a dead browser, abandoned by the folks in Redmond, Washington. So, it's likely not necessary to perform this little Houdini act on my style sheets. However, should someone hit a site I've designed with IE/Mac, this will ensure they'll get an unstyled view of the site, rather than a potentially broken-looking version of the intended visual design. I no longer test for or worry about designs in IE/Mac, so this hiding trick remains.

RESET.CSS

The first style sheet imported inside `screen.css` is a reset style sheet. Eric Meyer has been pioneering the concept of resetting the default styles that browsers apply to HTML elements by default. The reason is that these default styles often vary, depending on the browser. Resetting things before writing any of your own styles helps to start things from a consistent base.

There is also the benefit of not having to duplicate rules that are likely to be repeated throughout the style sheet. For example, while working on the CSS for MTV.com, we *didn't* use a reset style sheet, and I regret that. After doing a quick count of the number of times I used `margin: 0; padding: 0;` on various elements in order to zero things out, the final tally in the main style sheet for the site was somewhat staggering:

`margin: 0;` **66**

`padding: 0;` **89**

All told, that means there were **155** rules in the main style sheet that did nothing but zero out the default margins and padding that browsers apply. That's a lot of repetition.

I was late to the game in terms of using a reset style sheet—but now, after reevaluating my methods (sensing a trend here?) I've found it indispensable. And it's always imported *first*, ensuring the rest of the styles I write are on top of a consistent base.

TIP

My reset.css that I use as a base in every project is based on Eric Meyer's work, which can be found at http://meyerweb.com/eric/tools/css/reset.

```
/*
Title:    Reset default browser styles
Author:   dan@simplebits.com, based on Eric Meyer's Reset
➥CSS: http://meyerweb.com/eric/tools/css/reset
*/

html, body, div, span, applet, object, iframe, h1, h2, h3,
➥h4, h5, h6, p, blockquote, pre, a, abbr, acronym, address,
➥big, cite, code, del, dfn, em, font, img, ins, kbd, q,
```

```
⮑s, samp, small, strike, strong, sub, sup, tt, var, b, u,
⮑i, center, dl, dt, dd, ol, ul, li, fieldset, form, label,
⮑legend, table, caption, tbody, tfoot, thead, tr, th, td {
  margin: 0;
  padding: 0;
  font-size: 100%;
  vertical-align: baseline;
  border: 0;
  outline: 0;
  background: transparent;
  }

ol, ul {
  list-style: none;
  }

blockquote, q {
  quotes: none;
  }

:focus {
  outline: 0;
  }

table {
  border-collapse: collapse;
  border-spacing: 0;
  }
```

MASTER.CSS

After `reset.css` comes the feature presentation. The main course, `master.css`, contains all the site-specific styles for a given design. As a launching point, I have defined a few things in the framework to help quicken the pace.

Aside from base font styles and sizing, there are primarily just stubs for often-used elements that I anticipate including in the markup. Most sites have certain elements such as a header, footer, main content area, sidebar, and footer. So, having a commented spot for these in the style sheet saves a little time. By having the comments prepopulated here, I'm also setting a standard for comment formatting as well as separating the styles by location on the page going forward.

But most important, you'll notice that at the bottom, I have my `.group` clear fix already set up. It's there, ready to be used, to the point where I don't have to think of the CSS that's involved—only that using `.group` on a container will automagically clear floats within.

```css
/*
Title:    Master styles for screen media
Author:   dan@simplebits.com
*/

body {
  font-family: "Helvetica Neue", Helvetica, Arial,
↪sans-serif;
  color: #444;
  font-size: 62.5%;
  background: #fff;
  }

/* links */

a:link, a:visited {
  color: #369;
  outline: none;
  }
a:hover {
  color: #39c;
  }

/* page structure
------------------------------------------- */

#wrap {

  }
#main {

  }
#secondary {

  }
```

```
#footer {

  }

/* header
---------------------------------------- */

#logo {

  }

/* nav */

#nav {

  }

/* main styles
---------------------------------------- */


/* secondary styles
---------------------------------------- */


/* footer
---------------------------------------- */

#footer {

  }

/* misc.
---------------------------------------- */

hr, .hide {
  display: none;
  }
a img {
  border: none;
  }
```

(continued on next page)

```
/* self-clear floats */

.group:after {
  content: ".";
  display: block;
  height: 0;
  clear: both;
  visibility: hidden;
  }
```

IE.CSS

And finally, we import `ie.css`, which houses all the necessary hacks and patches to fix Internet Explorer. I like to quarantine these fixes into their own style sheet, thus keeping `master.css` clean and free of the ugly reality that is designing for the Web while still catering to IE's quirkiness.

In terms of the framework, you'll notice there's not much here—just a filter fix that can (sometimes) get background alpha-channel PNGs to display properly in IE6, and more important, the necessary fixes for auto-clearing floats in IE6 and IE7. Again, by reusing this framework for every project, I know I can count on the `.group` class to properly clear floats in all browsers. Set it and forget it.

```
/*
Title:    IE patches
Author:   dan@simplebits.com
*/

/* PNG fix */

* html #selector { /* for IE<6 */
  filter: progid:DXImageTransform.Microsoft.
➡AlphaImageLoader(enabled=true, sizingMethod=scale
➡src='img/image.png'); background-image: none; background-
➡repeat: no-repeat; background-color: transparent;
  }

/* self-clear floats */
```

```
* html .group { /* IE6 */
  height: 1%;
  }
*:first-child+html .group { /* IE7 */
  min-height: 1px;
  }
```

YOUR MILEAGE MAY VARY

While I've just walked through the structure of my own little CSS framework, it's not because I think it's the best available or even the most thorough, or that it'll work in every situation for every designer. Rather, I'm hoping it'll spark interest in building your own (if you don't use a framework already).

My framework is rather basic, and I could easily take it a bit further. But the key elements are in place here:

- Import a **reset style sheet** *first* to ensure a consistent base and save duplicating rules.

- Insert the **clear fix** declarations in master.css and ie.css to enable the .group class to be quickly applied whenever needed to contain floats in all browsers.

- **Quarantine hacks and patches** for Internet Explorer into their own style sheet.

Applying .group to Tugboat

Now that we have the framework in place, we can talk about the different areas of the Tugboat template where I've applied the .group clear fix, in order to see it in action.

Figure 5.10 (on the next page) shows an overlay of where I attached the .group class to preexisting markup. That is, I didn't need to add *extra* markup to aid in clearing floats, but rather added that .group class to containing elements that had floats within them. I could stay as semantic as possible in terms of the elements, ids, and class names that I chose, knowing that .group would handle the float containment.

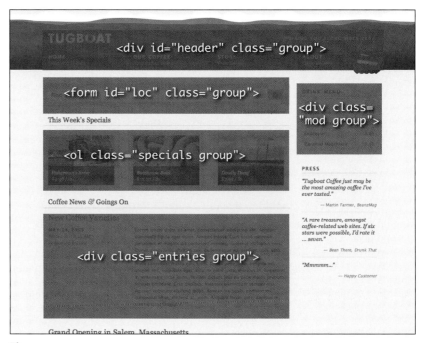

Figure 5.10

And this illustrates how the .group class can be added to an element that already has a class defining styles for it. For example, the "This Week's Specials" ordered list already had a class associated with it (<ol class="specials">) and I simply added .group at the end to handle the clear fixing.

MODULAR MOVES

So by ensuring floats are contained within their… *container*, we suddenly have a fully *modular* setup within our layouts. These individual chunks could even be moved around the page if necessary—without worrying about how that might affect other areas of the layout (**Figure 5.11**). The containers remain *independent modules*, where the floats that are necessary to achieve flexible layout remain in place but not escape their intended boundaries. A foundation for bulletproof design.

Figure 5.11 The Tugboat template with a few things shuffled around.

Wrapping Up

I've shared a reevaluation story of my own, as it relates to modular float management—but I'm hoping the takeaway from this chapter is that it could apply to a lot of the methods we use to create websites.

If being a craftsman involves continually asking questions along the way, then we started things off in Chapter 1 specifically asking, "What happens if…?" Another question posed here in the chapter could be, "Can the methods I'm currently using to create _____ be improved?"

In the opening quote, Dave Hoover argues that the experts wouldn't dare ask that of themselves but that craftsmen would *embrace* it, finding ways of refining and revising the way they build things. I wholeheartedly agree, and try my best to strive for better, more efficient ways of accomplishing the same goal, and remain unafraid to rethink and refine old habits.

6

The Fluid Grid

by Ethan Marcotte

The author invited renowned Web designer/
developer Ethan Marcotte to contribute this
insightful chapter to the book.

The Way is shaped by use,
But then the shape is lost.
Do not hold fast to shapes
But let sensation flow into the world
As a river courses down to the sea.

—Dao De Jing

In recent years, there's been a resurgence of interest in grid-based design and how it applies to the Web. As it turns out, the idea's a pretty old one, coming out of the world of print design from the early 20th century. Modernist designers of that time advocated that print design should be returned to a more type-centric style, stripped of pointless illustration and other subjective indulgences. They argued that all this ornamentation simply, well, got in the way—that all those pretty pictures hampered a design's ability to effectively communicate with its reader.

This eventually culminated in Josef Müller-Brockmann writing *Rastersysteme für die visuelle Gestaltung*, or *Grid Systems in Graphic Design*. In this book, Müller-Brockmann argued that a rigid grid system should be the foundation of every page layout. And the benefits were pretty clear: A modular framework of columns and rows would take some of the subjective guesswork out of the designer's hands, while enhancing the overall legibility of the design. Müller-Brockmann's own concert posters for the Tonhalle in Zürich epitomize this kind of geometric, type-heavy design, and are some of his best-known works (**Figure 6.1**).

Figure 6.1

Fast-forward a few decades, and we find the young field of "Web design" in a similar position. In the industry's early years, the relative newness of the technology—and the inadequacy of the browsers we designed for—made some of these more fundamental design principles feel like luxuries we designers couldn't afford. We spent half our time making sure dial-up connections weren't crying in pain, and the other half finding four ways to code the same website in every incompatible browser of the period. If that sounds like fun, it sort of was—in a very hectic, quasi-masochistic kind of way.

Of course, as browsers matured and support for Web standards flourished, the insanity gave way to exploration and experimentation. Sites like the CSS Zen Garden came to the forefront, and an army of standards-hungry designers leapt into the fray, Photoshop filters first.

Then, in late 2004 Khoi Vinh (**Figure 6.2**) and Mark Boulton (**Figure 6.3**) began arguing that designers needed to return to the basics; namely, that we had quite a lot to learn from the typographic grid, which is an artifact from the print world and one largely foreign to online design.

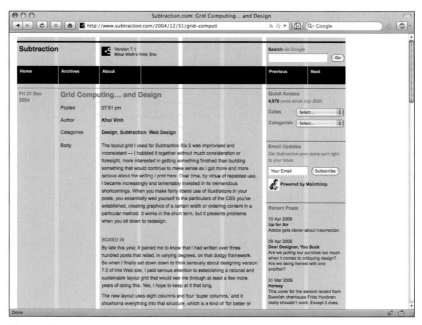

Figure 6.2

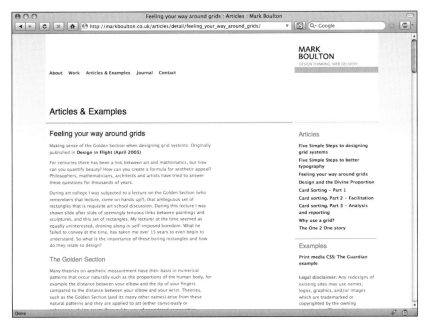

Figure 6.3

The Web design community seized upon the idea, and the grid has been something of a runaway success. Resource sites like The Grid System (http://www.thegridsystem.org/) sprang up overnight. A host of CSS frameworks such as Blueprint (http://www.blueprintcss.org/) and YUI Grids (http://developer.yahoo.com/yui/grids/) were created, all to make working with grids more accessible. So for now, a rational approach seems to be holding sway online, which benefits both designers *and* their users. Right?

There's only one slight problem. Nearly all of these grids are fixed, locked to a specific pixel width.

The Assignment

Nearly two years ago, the design firm I work for was approached by the World Wide Web Consortium (http://www.w3.org/) and asked to work on a redesign of the W3C site. It was a long and challenging project, in part because of the sheer amount of content developed and maintained on the site.

Design requirements from the client were pretty light. Since the W3C has such an information-dense website, our team was asked to focus on improving the site's legibility. So rather than clutter up the interface with overly designed elements, we took every step to ensure that the visual hierarchy of information was always well communicated by the typography. And after many months of collaboration with the client, a minimalist new design (**Figure 6.4**) was the result.

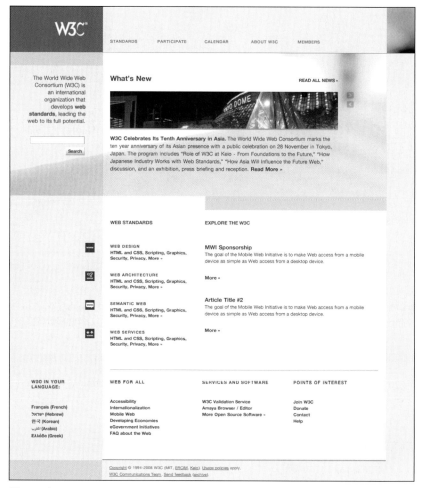

Figure 6.4

As you can see, the grid we ultimately settled on (**Figure 6.5**) divides the page into eight distinct columns, divided by even, measured gutters. The benefit for the designer, as it was in Müller-Brockmann's day, is that the grid becomes an invaluable layout tool: The columns gave us a framework for placing different elements on the page, and visually weighing them in relation to each other. But users also benefit, since the grid forms a set of natural lines to aid them as they read down the page, helping users better digest the reams of content found on the client's site.

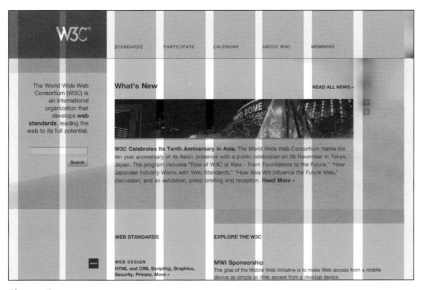

Figure 6.5

The other requirement we had was that the design had to be fluid, not fixed width. That way, as the window resized the design would automatically scale up or down to suit. Now normally the chance to work with a fluid layout would set my heart aflutter—I've been passionate about non-fixed designs ever since I started working online.

As for why I'm such a fan of fluid layouts—well, if it's okay with you, I'd like to tell you a brief story.

THE PROBLEM WITH FIXED WIDTH

I have a friend who works for a large research institution. She's a Web developer, and is one of the most tech-savvy people I've met. She knows a UNIX terminal like the back of her hand, helps scientists use software that parses data from satellites (I am not making this up), and can do illicit things with a Perl module. In her spare time, she relaxes with crossword puzzles, listens to podcasts while she cooks, and enjoys reading blogs, Twitter, and newspapers on her laptop.

But here's the thing: Her laptop's four or five years old, one that's been discontinued. It certainly works well enough, especially since she upgraded the memory and replaced its hard drive. But two things she can't replace are the screen and the video card. As a result, her display is locked to a screen resolution of 1024x768.

Geek that she is, this doesn't bother her. But I did notice something interesting when I first saw her reading one of her favorite online newspapers (**Figure 6.6**).

Figure 6.6

As you can see, she reserves space on the left for frequently used programs, and leaves a sliver of space on the right of her screen so that her desktop's still visible in case she needs to get her hands on a certain file. So while her screen may be set at a certain resolution, her browser window doesn't match it.

As a result, websites that assume a window width of around 1024 pixels don't fully fit in her window. The right-hand column frequently appears clipped, and on especially content-heavy pages, she's often missing cool stuff on the right. In fact, she's developed an interesting reading habit: She scrolls down a bit, then to the right, then back to the left, then down again. She zigzags in an L-pattern down the page, not because she's missing content but because she *might* be. Until she moves that scrollbar, she won't know what she's not seeing.

The problem with the fixed-width approach to interface design is that it's asking the user to adapt to the design rather than the reverse. My friend—and others like her—has to actively change her habits to suit the website, and misses scrollbar-concealed content when she fails to do so.

And it's not just the user who's penalized by a fixed-width layout. The site owners can potentially be affected as well (**Figure 6.7**).

Figure 6.7

The rightmost link in this screenshot says "Register Now." Presumably this is a fairly important link for the newspaper's business, bringing in new users, more eyeballs, and more clicks on advertisements. But its position on the page is pretty fragile—if the user is even slightly beneath the minimum screen resolution, they might miss that important call to action.

And the phrase "minimum screen resolution" is part of the problem. Fixed-width design is based on those three little words, which allow us to create an imaginary threshold for our users. With that in place, we create fixed-width websites, redesigning them every few years to raise the bar another monitor size or two. If our users and their browser windows meet that resolution threshold, then great; but if they don't, it's the scrollbar for them.

LESS SOAPBOX, MORE SOLUTIONS!

Of course, talk's pretty cheap. And when I was working on the W3C redesign, I didn't have the luxury of writing a multipage rant about the user-unfriendliness of fixed-width designs. Instead, I was faced with a sobering fact: Nearly all grid-based designs are fixed width, since designers felt that explicit pixel widths make complex, column-heavy layouts a cinch to code. So I had to figure out how to marry the rigidity of grid-based designs to the flexibility inherent in the Web. Is a "fluid grid" even feasible?

As it turns out, it is. Fluid grids are simply a matter of *context*.

Flexibility Through…Font Sizing?

Eventually, the solution came to me while I was working on another flexible aspect of the site's design: its typography. To better understand non-fixed-grid layouts, we'll take a few elements out of Dan's Tugboat design and conduct a little typesetting exercise. For instance, let's say Dan asked us to code up a comp with nothing but a section's headline, and a title and paragraph from a blog entry (**Figure 6.8**).

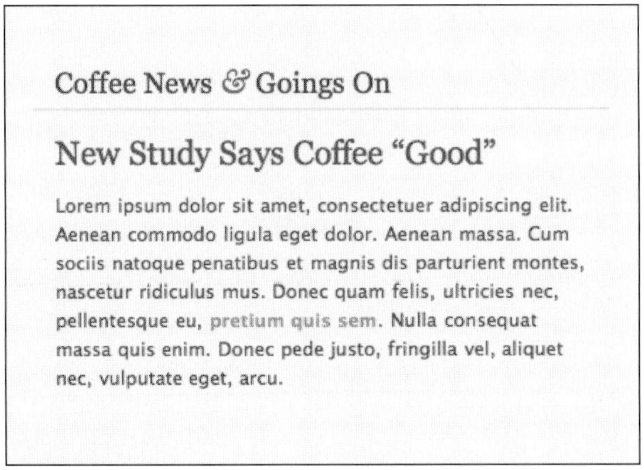

Coffee News *&* Goings On

New Study Says Coffee "Good"

Lorem ipsum dolor sit amet, consectetuer adipiscing elit. Aenean commodo ligula eget dolor. Aenean massa. Cum sociis natoque penatibus et magnis dis parturient montes, nascetur ridiculus mus. Donec quam felis, ultricies nec, pellentesque eu, pretium quis sem. Nulla consequat massa quis enim. Donec pede justo, fringilla vel, aliquet nec, vulputate eget, arcu.

Figure 6.8

This is one typelicious design we're looking at: simple, elegant, *legible* stuff. And while I'm not exactly sure what "typelicious" means, I do know that the markup for this section is pretty straightforward. We'll use a div to contain our main content area and another for the blog entry, with proper h2, h3, and p tags marking off the rest of the text, as best fits the *meaning* of the content we're marking up.

```
<div class="main">
  <h2>Coffee News <span class="amp">&amp;</span> Goings
➥On</h2>

  <div class="entry">
    <h3>New Study Says Coffee "Good"</h3>

    <div class="entry-body">
      <p>Lorem ipsum dolor sit amet, consectetuer…</p>
    </div><!-- /entry-body -->
```

```
    </div><!-- /entry -->
</div><!-- /main -->
```

Valid, semantically rich, and well structured—we're off to a good start. So with that foundation in place, let's apply a light layer of CSS to our plain-looking angle brackets.

```
body {
    font-size: 100%;
    font-family: "Lucida Grande", "Lucida Sans Unicode",
➥"Lucida Sans", Helvetica, Arial, sans-serif;
    font-weight: normal;
    background: #F3F2E8;
    color: #51463D;
}
```

Our `font-family` property says the browser should default to Lucida Grande if it's available, and then lists some backup typefaces if that font's not available. We've also applied a `background` of #F3F2E8 to the `body` element, and set a default color for our text (#51463D).

And finally, we've set a `font-size` value of 100%. Why 100%? We've simply set the base type size to the browser's default, which in most cases is 16 pixels. So if a user ever decided to bump up the browser's default font size a bit (**Figure 6.9**), the CSS would increase with her preference. But for our typesetting exercise, this gives us a solid baseline value to reference as we calculate the rest of our elements' type sizes.

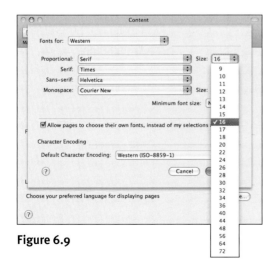

Figure 6.9

While I've written out three separate font properties (font-size, font-family, and font-weight), keep in mind that those can be collapsed into the shorthand font property, like so:

```
font: normal 100%
"Lucida Grande", "Lucida
Sans Unicode", "Lucida
Sans", Helvetica, Arial,
sans-serif;
```

So as you can see, we've done quite a bit of work with this single rule (**Figure 6.10**).

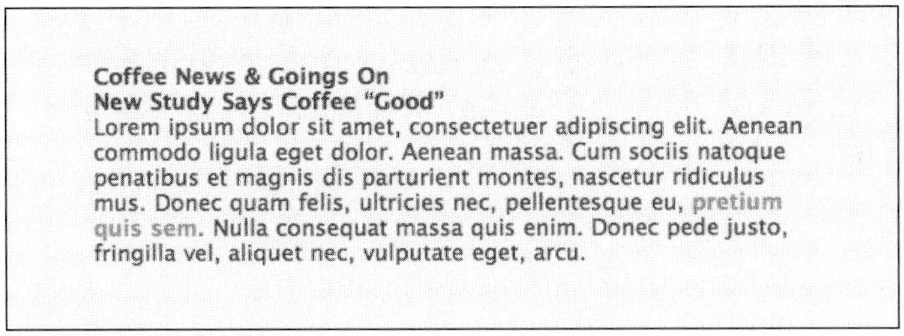

Figure 6.10

As Dan mentioned in the Introduction, we're using a reset.css file to, well, reset the browser's internal style sheet and zero out the default style rules it applies to HTML elements. That's why our headlines look so, well, un-headline-y. At the moment, all of our copy is set to the same font-size, inheriting the 100% value we set on the body. So in most cases, we can assume that this base value is 16 pixels, which we'll need as a reference point when we start working with relative font sizes.

A MATTER OF CONTEXT

Let's take a closer look at our comp to see what size and faces we should set our text in (**Figure 6.11**).

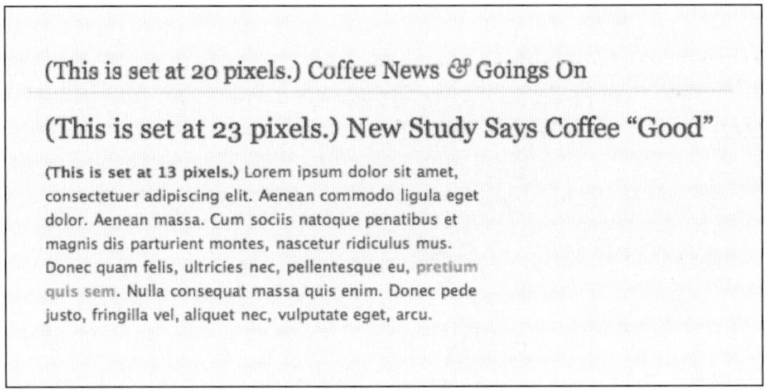

Figure 6.11

I've never been that smooth with the numbers—I blame the literature degree. For all the calculations in this section and beyond, I'm just using OS X's built-in Calculator program. Feel free to use any calculator-like program you like. Heck, an abacus would probably do the trick.

Speaking typographically, our work's pretty straightforward. The topmost headline and blog title are set in Georgia, at 20px and 23px respectively, while the entry's text is set at the default of 13px. Easy enough, right?

Well, this is where our ems come into play. When working with this relative unit, it's all about *context*. In other words, the actual size of an element's em is computed relative to the font-size of that element's parent. So to calculate our target font size value, we simply take the target font size value we want in pixels, and divide it by the font size of its container (that is, its context). The result we're left with is the desired font size, expressed in relative, scalable, wonderful ems:

```
target ÷ context = result
```

With this formula in hand, let's turn back to that headline. We know that we want to set it in 20px Georgia. And if we were setting it in pixels, it'd be easy enough:

```
.main h2 {
    font: normal 20px Georgia, serif;
}
```

However, 20px is just our *target* value. If we assume that the body, our *context,* has a base font-size of 16px, we can plug these two numbers into our formula:

```
20 ÷ 16 = 1.25
```

And there we have it: Our headline is 1.25 times the default body size, or 1.25em, which we can plug directly into our style rule.

```
.main h2 {
    font: normal 1.25em Georgia, serif;
    /* 20px / 16px = 1.25em */
}
```

With that, our headline nicely matches the typography laid out in the design, and is user-resizable to boot (**Figure 6.12**). So far, so good.

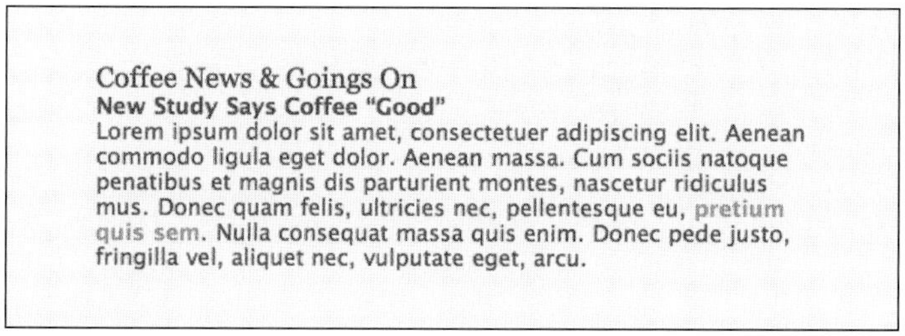

> Coffee News & Goings On
> **New Study Says Coffee "Good"**
> Lorem ipsum dolor sit amet, consectetuer adipiscing elit. Aenean commodo ligula eget dolor. Aenean massa. Cum sociis natoque penatibus et magnis dis parturient montes, nascetur ridiculus mus. Donec quam felis, ultricies nec, pellentesque eu, pretium quis sem. Nulla consequat massa quis enim. Donec pede justo, fringilla vel, aliquet nec, vulputate eget, arcu.

Figure 6.12

But we're not quite done; our blog title and entry need some em love as well. Thankfully, we can use our `target ÷ context = result` formula on them as well. Since the title is set at 23px Georgia in the design, we simply plug this new target value into our formula:

```
23 ÷ 16 = 1.4375
```

And for our lonely paragraph, which is set at 13px:

```
13 ÷ 16 = 0.8125
```

Sure, that's a lot of decimal places. But nonetheless, those are the font size values we're after: Our entry title is 1.4375 times greater than the font size of the body, the entry itself 0.8125 times smaller. And those em-based values will fit nicely into our style sheet, like so:

```
div.entry h3 {
  font: normal 1.4375em/1.3 Georgia, serif;
  /* 23px / 16px = 1.4375em */
}
```

```
div.entry-body {
  font-size: 0.8125em;
  /* 13px / 16px = 0.8125 */
  line-height: 1.6;
}
```

Again, we're just describing the font size of these elements relative to the font size of their containing element, which in this case is the `font-size: 100%` we set on the `body`. And now that we've done so, our three elements are finally sized properly (**Figure 6.13**).

Figure 6.13

The Fluid Grid   145

But wait—that ampersand isn't looking quite right. If we look at Dan's
mockup (**Figure 6.14**), his looks, well, much nicer.

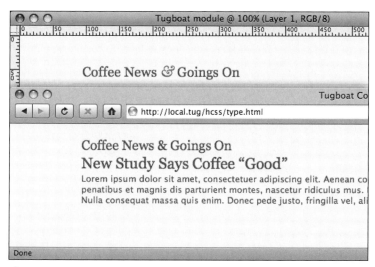

Figure 6.14

In Dan's comp, the ampersand is a gorgeous Baskerville italic, sized at 24px,
which sets it apart nicely from the rest of the headline. Our ampersand, on
the other hand, is just inheriting the 23px Georgia from our h2. So obviously,
our typesetting's not quite done.

CHANGING OUR CONTEXT

So, Baskerville at 24 pixels? Well, if we were just bringing over pixel-based
values from our comp, the CSS would look like this:

```
span.amp {
  font: normal 24px Baskerville, "Goudy Old Style",
➥"Palatino", "Book Antiqua", serif;
  font-style: italic;
  color: #766557;
}
```

But as with the rest of our typesetting, we want to express our font-size in
relative terms, not hard pixel values. So as before, we'll need to haul out our
trusty target ÷ context = result formula.

However, one important thing has changed. Until now, we've been using a context of 16px—the `font-size` set on the `body`—for all of our other elements. But now, the ampersand we want to style is actually *inside* another element:

```
<h2>Coffee News <span class="amp">&amp;</span> Goings On</h2>
```

If our `<h2>` didn't have an explicit `font-size` on it, we could still use 16px in our formula. But since we've declared a `font-size` on the headline, our context has changed, and we need to express the size of any child elements in relation to `1.25em`, or `20px`.

To do so, we can simply plug our desired target of `24px` into our formula, using `20px` as the context:

```
24 ÷ 20 = 1.2
```

And there we have it: our ampersand needs to be 1.2 times greater than the font size of its containing headline, or `1.2em`. We can drop that value directly into our `span.amp` rule:

```
span.amp {
  font: normal 1.2em Baskerville, "Goudy Old Style",
➥"Palatino", "Book Antiqua", serif;
  /* 24px / 20px = 1.2em */
  font-style: italic;
  color: #766557;
}
```

And at last, our elements are finally shaping up properly, appearing in their proper sizes and typefaces (**Figure 6.15**).

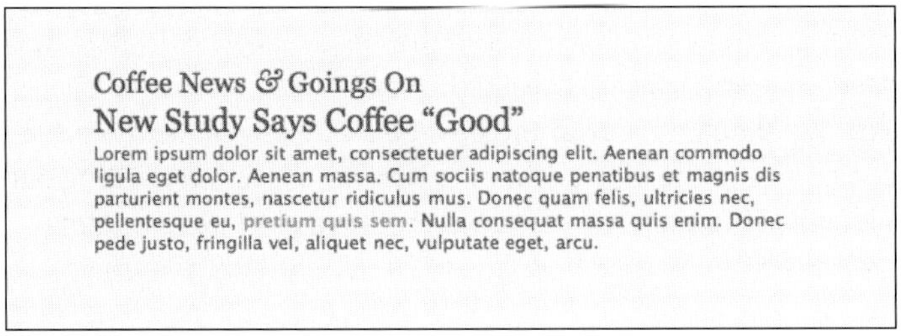

Figure 6.15

With that last flourish in place, all our text is sized properly, and is set in the intended typefaces. And with some minor cleanup—a splash of color here, a bit of `line-height` there—the page is finally in line with Dan's design (**Figure 6.16**).

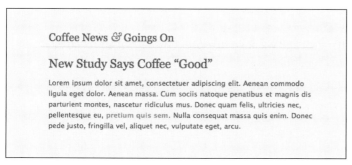

Figure 6.16

So our little text module's finally done—it's typeset beautifully, and using relative, resize-friendly ems.

WAX ON, WAX OFF

At this point, you might be wondering where that Cederholm fellow found the shmoe who's writing this chapter. After all, he's supposed to be talking about *page layouts*. Why on earth is he prattling on about relative font sizes? (Also, he's kind of shifty-eyed, and I'm pretty sure he just stole a few bucks out of petty cash. Better call security.)

But it was when I was working on the em-based typography for the W3C redesign that it hit me: Every aspect of a grid, and the elements placed within it, can be expressed as a proportion relative to its container. As when we size type for the Web, we shouldn't look at the desired size of an element but *the relationship of that size to the element's container*. So rather than setting our columns in rigid, inflexible pixels, we can convert those pixel-based widths into percentage-based values, which will keep the proportions of the grid intact as it resizes.

In other words, we'll have a fluid grid. Let's try it out.

Mo' Fluid, Mo' Grids, Mo' Betta

To create the proportions needed for a flexible, non-fixed grid, let's start with another simplified Tugboat comp (**Figure 6.17**). All we've done here is widen the scope a bit: We've added a sidebar to the right, and a footer to the bottom of the page; beneath our blog entry's title, we've added some meta-information on the left, and shifted the entry itself over to the right to better accommodate it.

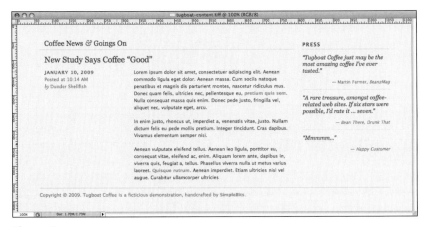

Figure 6.17

Thankfully, we don't need to change our markup all that much. We can recycle the HTML from our typesetting example, and add in an unordered list for the entry's meta-information (`<ul class="entry-meta">`), with new containing blocks for our sidebar (`<div class="secondary">`) and footer (`<div id="footer">`). And then we can wrap the whole thing in, well, `<div id="wrap">`.

```
<div id="wrap" class="group">

  <div class="main">
    <h2>Coffee News <span class="amp">&amp;</span> Goings
➡On</h2>

    <div class="entry last group">
      <h3>New Study Says Coffee "Good"</h3>

      <ul class="entry-meta">
        <li><h4>January 10, 2009</h4></li>
```

```
      <li>Posted at 10:14 <abbr>AM</abbr></li>
      <li><span class="by">by</span> Dunder Shellfish</li>
    </ul>

    <div class="entry-body">
      <p>Lorem ipsum dolor sit amet, consectetur...</p>
    </div><!-- /entry-body -->
  </div><!-- /entry -->
</div><!-- /main -->

<div class="secondary">
  <div class="mod alt">
    <h3>Press</h3>

    <ul class="press">
      <li>
        <blockquote>
          <p>"Tugboat Coffee just may be the most amazing
➥coffee I've ever tasted."</p>
          <p class="author">- Martin Farmer,
➥<cite>BeanzMag</cite></p>
        </blockquote>
      </li>
      <li>...</li>
    </ul>
  </div>
</div> <!-- /secondary -->

<div id="footer">
  Copyright © 2009.  Tugboat Coffee is a fictitious
➥demonstration, handcrafted by <a href="http://simplebits.
➥com/">SimpleBits</a>.
  </div> <!-- /footer -->
</div> <!-- /wrap -->
```

During our little design exercise, let's suppose that all the tricky typography stuff's already been sorted. For the next few sections, we'll assume that we've gotten our serifs in place and our lines neatly leaded, and the only thing left to tackle is, well, the layout. As a result, our design is looking beautifully typeset—but a little too linear (**Figure 6.18**).

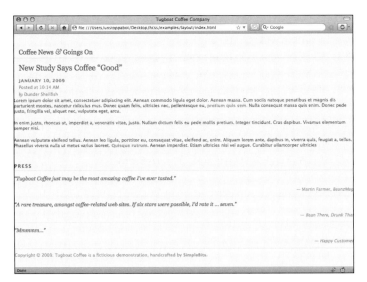

Figure 6.18

So to get started with our first fluid grid, let's take a closer look at the design.

FROM MOCKUP TO MARKUP

Generally speaking, the grid Dan's based the design on is very straightforward. The page is 1,000 pixels wide in the mockup, with four equal-width columns of 250 pixels each (**Figure 6.19**). The grid's a little irregular in that there aren't any margins between the individual columns, but that doesn't stop the design from looking *good*.

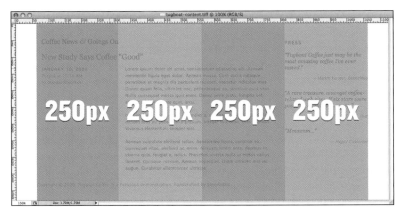

Figure 6.19

Continuing with our visual inventory, we can see that the large content blocks (which we've already marked up with `<div class="main">` and `<div class="secondary">`, if you'll remember), are draped nicely across those four columns. The sidebar's stationed firmly on the right, covering one column at a width of 250 pixels. But since `<div class="main">` should be, well, the main area of focus, Dan allocated the most space to it on the grid. It spans three of the columns, less the 20-pixel-wide right-hand margin that Dan's wisely left between it and the sidebar. All of this tallies up to a total width of 730 pixels for our main content area (**Figure 6.20**).

Figure 6.20

So if we were simply coding another fixed-width site, we could snap most of this into place pretty quickly with three simple rules:

```
#wrap {
  margin: 0 auto;
  padding: 40px 0 0 0;
  width: 1000px;
}

.main {
  float: left;
  width: 730px;
}

.secondary {
  float: right;
  width: 250px;
}
```

We've given our containing #wrap block a width of 1000px and centered the design horizontally using margin: 0 auto;. Within that block, we've floated our `<div class="secondary">` sidebar off to the right and given it a `width` of 250px. Our `.main` block, however, is floated to the left, and set to the `width` of 730px that the comp calls for.

So if pixels were our thing, we'd be almost done with our layout. Of course, those fixed widths don't quite cut the proverbial mustard. Even at window widths of 1024x768, it doesn't take much for a scrollbar to appear (**Figure 6.21**). Instead, we need to describe those column widths as *percentages*, not pixels. But how do we do that?

Figure 6.21

DIVISION SIGN DÉJÀ VU

That's right—it's the return of our old friend, the `target ÷ context = result` formula. But instead of font sizes, we can use this kind of proportional analysis to turn our pixel-based columns into percentage-based, *flexible* ones. This will leave us with a grid-based design built on proportions, not pixels—and those proportions will scale as our users' windows do.

Rethinking the wrap

Let's start with our containing element, the eponymous #wrap:

```
#wrap {
  margin: 0 auto;
  padding: 40px 0 0 0;
  width: 1000px;
}
```

Rather than assign an explicit width to #wrap, let's give it a max-width instead. I like to think of max-width as a fine compromise for the flexible-minded designer: It allows the design to scale *down* if the user's window doesn't meet our "minimum screen resolution" threshold, but allows the designer (that's you!) to set the "optimal" viewing width for your design, and thus prevent lines of text from getting overly long.

Now, we could easily set our max-width in pixels, like so:

```
#wrap {
  margin: 0 auto;
  padding: 40px 0 0 0;
  max-width: 1000px;
}
```

However, a pixel-based max-width can look pretty weird on larger displays. Someone viewing the design on a very large monitor would get a ton of unnecessary white space on either side of our design. So while that may not be a *huge* usability issue, there's another, better way: Instead of pixels, let's use our good friend, the em.

Just as we did with our typesetting exercise, we can convert that pixel-based max-width of 1000px into an em-based width. And as we did before, we simply need to look at the context we're working in. Remember the font-size we set on the body?

```
body {
  font-size: 100%;
  font-family: "Lucida Grande", "Lucida Sans Unicode",
➡"Lucida Sans", Helvetica, Arial, sans-serif;
  font-weight: normal;
  background: #F3F2E8;
  color: #51463D;
}
```

As you know by now, our font-size: 100% is roughly equivalent to 16 pixels in most browsers. So to get a *target* value of 1000px on #wrap, we simply need to divide it by our *context* of 16 to get an em-based *result*:

```
1000 / 16 = 62.5
```

There we are: 62.5em will roughly work out to 1000px for our max-width, which we can drop neatly into our #wrap rule.

NOTE

Some accessibility-minded designers consider max-width to be problematic, arguing that there is no such thing as an "ideal" line length. As a result, they claim that designers shouldn't place any constraint on their users (see http://projectcerbera.com/web/articles/line-lengths and http://accessifyforum.com/viewtopic.php?p=65693#65693). I leave the decision up to the reader, but our design would work just fine without max-width; the fluid grid technique doesn't rely on it at all.

NOTE

Many modern browsers like Firefox 3, Opera, and Safari now default to an Opera-like "page zoom." Instead of just increasing the size of the design's fonts, those browsers will scale the entire design—images, embedded media, the works—up with the text. Even Internet Explorer 8 ships with this feature! So while em-based max-widths may not be strictly necessary for the latest 'n' greatest browsers, they still place an additional level of control in the hands of our users, especially those using slightly older browsers.

```
#wrap {
  margin: 0 auto;
  padding: 40px 0 0 0;
  max-width: 62.5em;
}
```

With an em-based `max-width` in place, the user can easily increase the size of the design by bumping up her browser's text, which will come in handy at higher resolutions. And of course, since we're not setting an explicit `width` on our `#wrap` container, it will just resize automatically if the user's on a smaller display. Hooray for fluid containers!

From the outside, in

Now that we've gotten rid of the pixel-based width on `#wrap`, let's turn to the two content containers immediately beneath it: `.main` and `.secondary`.

```
.main {
  float: left;
  width: 730px;
}
```

```
.secondary {
  float: right;
  width: 250px;
}
```

Even though we've given `#wrap` a flexible, em-based `max-width`, we can still use the dimensions outlined in Dan's comp as our guide. We have a width of 730px for `.main`, contained within a 1000px-wide container—and if we plug those values into our `target ÷ context = result` container, we'll have our flexible width.

730 ÷ 1000 = .73

So `.73`, or 73%, is the width we need for `.main`. Can we do the same for `.secondary`?

250 ÷ 1000 = .25

And voilà! If we move the decimal over a few places, we've got a `width` of 25%. So let's update our CSS with those new values:

```
.main {
  float: left;
  width: 73%;
}

.secondary {
  float: right;
  width: 25%;
}
```

Finally, we've got the makings of a real fluid grid (**Figure 6.22**). With our two percentage-based columns in place, the *proportions* of our design are always intact, even as it reflows to fit within the user's browser window.

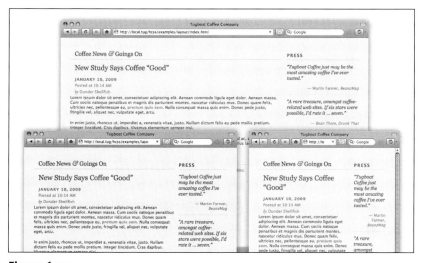

Figure 6.22

COLUMNS, CONTEXT, AND CHANGES—OH MY!

On the highest level, our fluid grid is shaping up nicely: we've got an em-based max-width set on our #wrap container, and two percentage-based columns that are sized in proportion to it. To finish up our design, then, we need to turn our attention to the blog entry and the new metadata list to the left of it.

So as before, let's take a closer look at our comp (**Figure 6.23**), and see what needs to be built.

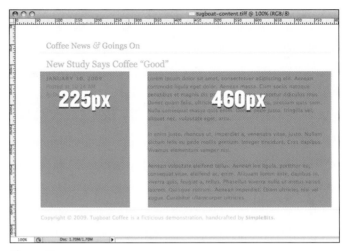

Figure 6.23

In the design, our metadata (<ul class="entry-meta">) sits in the leftmost column and is only 225 pixels wide. The entry (<div class= "entry-body">) itself, however, has been set to 460px, and is draped across the second two columns to the right.

Once again, if we were satisfied with mere pixels (I hope you can hear the scorn in my voice), two simple rules would snap this design into place pretty easily:

```
div.entry ul.entry-meta {
  float: left;
  width: 225px;
}

div.entry-body {
  float: right;
  width: 460px;
  font-size: 1em;
  line-height: 1.6;
}
```

But we're a couple dozen pages into this chapter, and I feel like you guys really know me by now. We don't, as the kids say, *need no stinkin' pixels.*

However, before we can haul out our old proportional formula, we should find out what our context is. Just as when we `font-size`d our ampersand relative to its containing headline, we're no longer dealing with the `1000px`-wide `#wrap` block. Instead, we need to find out the widths of `ul.entry-meta` and `div.entry-body` relative to their container, `.main` (**Figure 6.24**).

Figure 6.24

Since `.main` is sized at 730 pixels in the comp, we now have our context value. Because we need to express the width of `ul.entry-meta`—225px—as a percentage of `730px`, it's back to the old formula:

`225 ÷ 730 = 0.30822`

This gives us a value of 0.30822, or 30.822%. And for `div.entry-body`, which is set at `460px` in the comp?

`460 ÷ 730 = 0.63014`

There we are: `div.entry-body` is 63.014% of its container, `div.main`. Without further ado (or further division), let's drop those values into our CSS:

```css
div.entry ul.entry-meta {
  float: left;
  width: 30.822%;
}

div.entry-body {
  float: right;
  width: 63.014%;
  font-size: 1em;
  line-height: 1.6;
}
```

And finally, our fluid grid is complete (**Figure 6.25**). High five! At long last, we've cracked that old chestnut: Page layouts are no longer the domain of the rigidly fixed width. Instead, we can create complex, column-rich, *grid-based* designs that scale along with the user's preferences.

Figure 6.25

But don't pop the champagne corks quite yet. While it's true we've got a modular, scalable layout framework in place, the designs we've been working from have, well, been a little skewed in our favor. Up until now, we've been a bit spoiled by the complete lack of fixed-width media. That's right: Our design's devoid of anything that *isn't* text.

Is a fluid interface designer's work *ever* done?

Fluid Media

Thankfully, it almost is. Although it's true that fixed-width media can make it more challenging to manage a flexible design, it's definitely not impossible, especially compared to everything we've done so far in this book. All it takes is some careful math, some percentage-based widths, and (you guessed it) the return of our handy proportion formula.

THIS AIN'T YOUR MAMA'S IMG TAG

Let's say we want to incorporate a photo into our blog post; I've found this beautiful, Creative Commons-licensed photo of a mouth-watering cappuccino (**Figure 6.26**) posted on Flickr.

Figure 6.26

So with a gorgeous-looking photo at the ready, let's clear a space for it in our markup:

```
<div class="entry">
  <h3>New Study Says Coffee "Good"</h3>

  <ul class="entry-meta">
    <li><h4>January 10, 2009</h4></li>
    <li>Posted at 10:14 <abbr>AM</abbr></li>
    <li><span class="by">by</span> Dunder Shellfish</li>
  </ul>

  <div class="entry-body">
    <p class="photo"><img src="coffee.jpg" alt="" /></p>
    <p>Lorem ipsum dolor sit amet, consectetuer…</p>
  </div><!-- /entry-body -->
</div><!-- /entry -->
```

Nothing fancy: We've dropped the img element for our cleverly named coffee.jpg into a paragraph at the top of our entry, and given it a class of photo.

Now, you may have noticed that the copy of Alexander's photo I downloaded weighs in at 1,024 pixels wide and 681 pixels tall. So in Web-speak, it's a little huge. However, before we bust out the image editor to resize it down, let's take a look at our page as is (**Figure 6.27**).

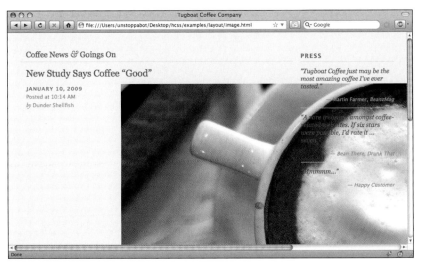

Figure 6.27

Oof. Well, *that's* pretty awful. Since there's nothing actively constraining its ginormous dimensions, the image simply overflows its containing paragraph. So as it stands, our image simply won't do.

However, what if we *did* constrain the dimensions of coffee.jpg somehow? In fact, what if we wrote a CSS rule that says that *all* images should never exceed the width of their container?

Drop this into your CSS, and your woes should be decidedly resolved:

```
img {
  max-width: 100%;
}
```

By setting a `max-width: 100%;` on all images in our document, we're setting a very abstract restriction on them. They're allowed to render at their native width and height, as long as their width doesn't exceed that of their containing element. So with that single rule, images will scale up or down proportionally as their containers do, and our layout is fixed once again (**Figure 6.28**).

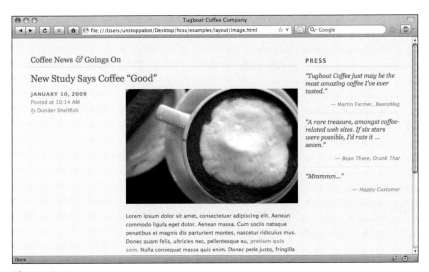

Figure 6.28

We can even modify a style Dan wrote earlier, and give the paragraph that supremely hot rounded border effect from Chapter 2.

```
img {
  max-width: 100%;
}

p.photo {
  border: 15px solid #e2e1d4;
  background: #e2e1d4;
  border: 15px solid #e2e1d4;
  border-radius: 8px;
  -webkit-border-radius: 8px;
  -moz-border-radius: 8px;
}
```

Hot coffee, hot border effects, together at last. And all scaling wonderfully in Dan's design (**Figure 6.29**).

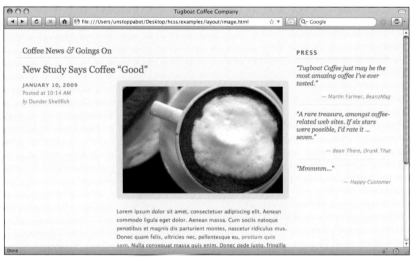

Figure 6.29

The other wonderful thing about our max-width: 100% approach to constraining images is that it can easily apply to other types of fixed-width media. For example, if you're inserting a Flash object into your markup, we can simply extend our rule a bit further.

```
img,
object {
    max-width: 100%;
}
```

It's as simple as that. Modern browsers have evolved to a point where they can intelligently scale fixed media proportionally, with a little bit of max-width instruction from our style sheets.

Well, *most* browsers have. Others require a bit of tough love.

IE AND ITS DECIDEDLY IMPERFECT CSS IMPLEMENTATION, SITTING IN A TREE…

As you may well be aware, there's no support for max-width in Internet Explorer before version 7. So as much as we'd like to forget that IE6 ever happened, the browser still holds a significant portion of today's market share.

TIP

Use sIFR for custom typography on your website? You'll be pleased to know that recent builds of sIFR 3 support fluid and flexible layouts right out of the box, reflowing the text automatically as the titles' containers resize. See it in action on my blog (http://unstoppable robotninja.com), and get a recent build of sIFR 3 at http:// wiki.novemberborn.net/sifr3/.

But does that lack of `max-width` support mean we're up the proverbial creek without a proverbial paddle?

Quite proverbially, no. Instead, we can simply insert the following into an IE-specific style sheet.

```
img,
object {
  width: 100%;
}
```

Now, this is a very different rule than our `max-width: 100%` directive, and requires a bit of caution: Instead of setting an upper limit for our image, this other rule simply sets the width of our elements to the width of their container.

While this will work well for images like our `coffee.jpg`, which we can reliably assume to always be too large for its containing element, smaller images might get stretched up, causing some distortion. So if you know areas of your markup that will consistently have oversized, fluid layout-friendly media, you might add some additional specificity into your selectors in order to properly quarantine the rule. For example:

```
img.full,
p.photo img,
object.full {
  width: 100%;
}
```

This added level of specificity effectively limits the scope of the `width: 100%` rule, ensuring that it doesn't cause any weird up-scaling in any problematic areas of your design. But when safely applied, it's a great workaround for the nonexistent `max-width` support in older versions of Internet Explorer.

So that settles the issue, right? Well... mostly. Strictly speaking, our next bug isn't IE-specific, but it is *Windows*-specific.

(You're excited. I can tell.)

A PROBLEM OF PLATFORMS (WELL, ONE PLATFORM)

If you look at our page layout with Firefox 2 on Windows, or any version of Internet Explorer, our CSS-resized `coffee.jpg` might look a little broken. As it turns out, Windows doesn't scale images particularly well. They look heavily artifacted when they're resized, and the quality of highly detailed images—especially those with text in them—can suffer.

I've prepared a quick test case to demonstrate this. I took a screenshot of the text from an old blog entry of mine and dropped it into a large image. I'm resizing that image with the `max-width: 100%;` rule we wrote earlier, substituting `width: 100%` for IE6 and below. Even in IE7 (**Figure 6.30**), the loss of quality is pretty drastic.

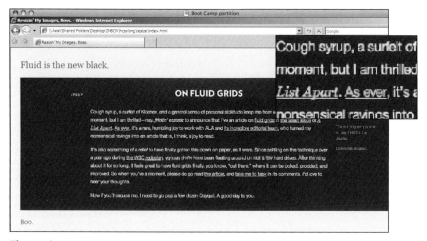

Figure 6.30

As you can see, the text is almost broken in IE7 (**Figure 6.31**), which makes this a pretty severe bug. Scalable images are great and all, but not if the quality of the content inside them will suffer as a result.

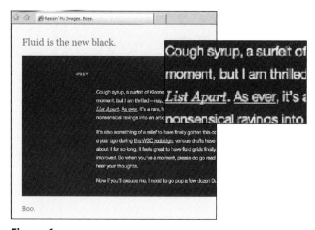

Figure 6.31

Thankfully, this problem is limited to all versions of Internet Explorer, as well as Firefox 2 (and below) on Windows. Safari/Win (Safari on Windows), Opera/Win, and Firefox 3/Win are all just fine and scale our images properly. So before we toss our fluid framework out with the bathwater (and a few other mixed metaphors), let's focus on the affected browsers and see what we can do.

First, the bad news.

Firefox 2 on Windows, we hardly knew ye

Unfortunately, the Firefox 2 bug is one we'll have to live with. The JavaScript required in order to target older versions of Firefox, and just on Windows, is unreliable at best. But more importantly, Firefox 2 doesn't have any hidden mechanism to repair its image rendering. If there was a toggle to, say, kick its image rendering into high gear, we'd be able to repair the issue. But it doesn't, so we can't.

The good news here is that most Firefox users are pretty diligent about upgrading, and Firefox 2's an increasingly rare browser. So while the lack of a workable solution is less than ideal, hopefully the absence of an "improved rendering toggle" won't impact too many of our users.

But hey—as it turns out, Internet Explorer *does* have such a toggle. Who knew?

IE's proprietary CSS filters to the rescue! (Wait, did I just type that?)

One long-standing issue with Internet Explorer 6 and below is its inability to handle PNGs—or, more specifically, the proper alpha transparency provided by PNG files. To work around this, designers have relied on a proprietary Microsoft CSS filter called `AlphaImageLoader` (http://msdn.microsoft.com/en-us/library/ms532969.aspx). So if you had a PNG background on your `#logo div`, you could drop the following into your IE-specific style sheet to clear up the transparency problem:

```
#logo a {
  background: none;
  filter: progid:DXImageTransform.Microsoft.
➥AlphaImageLoader(src="/path/to/bg.png",
➥sizingMethod="scale");
}
```

NOTE

There have been a number of JavaScript functions written to fix PNG transparency in `img` elements as well. Drew McClellan's SuperSleight (http://24ways.org/2007/supersleight-transparent-png-in-ie6) is a personal favorite. Though most recently I've been using the DD_belatedPNG library (http://www.dillerdesign.com/experiment/DD_belatedPNG/), which offers more flexibility than `AlphaImageLoader`-based hacks.

Now, who knows what *really* happens under the IE hood. But essentially, three different things are occurring here:

1. The PNG we'd applied to the background of `#logo` is removed.

2. The image is inserted into an `AlphaImageLoader` object, which sits "between" the background layer and the `div`'s content.

3. The `sizingMethod` property (http://msdn.microsoft.com/en-us/library/ms532920(VS.85).aspx) dictates whether the image inside the `AlphaImageLoader` object should `crop` the image to the dimensions of its container, treat it as a regular `image`, or `scale` it to fit its containing element.

What's this have to do with our rendering issue? Well, when I was working on the W3C redesign, I discovered that applying `AlphaImageLoader` to an image drastically improved its rendering quality in IE—or at least, brought it up to par with other, less unfortunate browsers. As it happens, I've written some JavaScript that automates this process, which I've included here:

```
var imgSizer = {
  Config : {
    spacer : "/path/to/your/spacer.gif",
    imgCache : []
  }

  ,collate : function(oScope) {
    if (document.all && !window.opera) {
      var c = imgSizer;
      var imgCache = c.Config.imgCache;

      var images = (oScope && oScope.length) ? oScope :
➥document.getElementsByTagName("img");
      for (var i = 0; i < images.length; i++) {
        images[i].origWidth = images[i].offsetWidth;
        images[i].origHeight = images[i].offsetHeight;

        imgCache.push(images[i]);
        c.ieAlpha(images[i]);
        images[i].style.width = "100%";
      }

      if (imgCache.length) {
        c.resize(function() {
```

```
        for (var i = 0; i < imgCache.length; i++) {
            var ratio = (imgCache[i].offsetWidth /
➥imgCache[i].origWidth);
            imgCache[i].style.height = (imgCache[i].
➥origHeight * ratio) + "px";
        }
    });
  }
 }
}

  ,ieAlpha : function(img) {
    var c = imgSizer;
    if (img.oldSrc) {
      img.src = img.oldSrc;
    }
    var src = img.src;
    img.style.width = img.offsetWidth + "px";
    img.style.height = img.offsetHeight + "px";
    img.style.filter = "progid:DXImageTransform.Microsoft.
➥AlphaImageLoader(src='" + src + "', sizingMethod='scale')"
    img.oldSrc = src;
    img.src = c.Config.spacer;
  }

  ,resize : function(func) {
    var oldonresize = window.onresize;
    if (typeof window.onresize != 'function') {
      window.onresize = func;
    } else {
      window.onresize = function() {
        if (oldonresize) {
          oldonresize();
        }
        func();
      }
    }
  }
}
```

The only customization you'll need to do is to change the spacer path (the third line from the top) to point to a transparent, 1x1 GIF on your website, and you'll be set. Simply invoke it once the page loads, and it'll soup up every image on the page for you. Personally, I prefer using Simon Willison's addLoadEvent() (http://simonwillison.net/2004/May/26/addLoadEvent/) to queue up functions to fire when the page loads, which might look like this:

```
<script type="text/javascript">
addLoadEvent(function() {
  imgSizer.collate();
});
</script>
```

As with our width: 100% hack for IE, the imgSizer.collate(); will scrub *all* images in your document and apply the AlphaImageLoader hack. In case that's a bit too broad for you, the function can also accept a collection of img elements, like so:

```
<script type="text/javascript">
addLoadEvent(function() {
  var oImgs = document.getElementById("wrap").
➥getElementsByTagName("img");
  imgSizer.collate(oImgs);
});
</script>
```

NOTE

Not a big fan of typing all that code out? Can't say I blame you. For the copy-and-paste fans out there, I recently blogged about this technique (http://unstoppablerobotninja. com/entry/fluid-images/), and provided the script for download. Have fun!

But no matter how you apply the fix, the benefits of the AlphaImageLoader workaround are pretty clear.

Our test case is finally fixed (**Figure 6.32**). Compare a detailed view of the text before and after the fix is applied (**Figure 6.33**), and I'm sure you'll agree that even though it's a nasty bit of proprietary code, the quality of the resized image makes it all worthwhile. And furthermore, our last little hurdle to truly flexible, fluid websites is cleared.

Figure 6.32

Figure 6.33

Wrapping Up

Goodness. It's been a journey of a chapter, hasn't it? We've reviewed the myriad tools available to the flexible-minded Web designer, and constructed a modular yet *fluid* grid. But is it all just theory? Is anyone actually using this stuff?

Well, as it turns out, both of your humble authors are (**Figure 6.34**). And as part of the W3C redesign effort we worked on, our firm did come up with a suite of production-ready templates for their website, all based on a bulletproof fluid grid. I'm firmly convinced that fluid layouts are ready for prime time, and I hope that we've found a few ways to fire up your non-fixed imagination.

Figure 6.34

But should you take all of this to mean that fixed-width design is bad? Far from it. I do, however, think it's time we recognize that our users' browsing habits aren't as fixed as our Photoshop comps might suggest. As we've seen in this chapter, the tools to scale our designs are easily available—we just need to move beyond our reliance on "minimum screen resolution."

Once we do, our users will thank us for it.

7

Craftsmanship Details

A bold architectural statement turns a public building into a landmark, but it is in the details where the architect becomes the real storyteller.

—Curtis W. Fentress, Architect

While Curtis Fentress is referring to architecture in the *physical* sense in the opening quote, we can apply his thinking to Web design as well. You've likely heard "The devil is in the details," but Fentress emphasizes that details are crucial (and positive) to the *storytelling* of architecture. I couldn't agree more; on the Web, implementing design involves a cacophony of details, and applying precious time to the *appropriate* details is what elevates your site to great design.

I'm going to spend this final chapter talking about several more details in relation to our tried and true Tugboat template. Most of these are fun, and all of them will prove useful. Like the details of craftsmanship, these last examples are often not obvious to everyone—but their presence further strengthens the design, site, and message. And it's those types of details I get most excited about.

Let's get things started with a little typography trick that will eventually lead us further into the world of type on the Web.

Use the Best Possible Ampersand

Typography is *essential* in designing for the Web. And for me it's the Web itself that's fueled a continuing interest in the field of typography. Think about it: What's a website without hypertext? It's a free and abundant resource on the Web, and it's how we (and websites) communicate online. So, attention to the craft of typography can go a long way in creating meaningful interfaces.

Jeffrey Zeldman writes in "Understanding Web Design" (www.alistapart.com/articles/understandingwebdesign):

> If one must compare the Web to other media, typography would be a better choice. For a Web design, like a typeface, is an environment for someone else's expression.

Here, Jeffrey is comparing the Web design as a whole to that of a typographer. Every website has a goal, message, or action, but its visual design or presentation might differ—just as a typeface may use the same letters to create vastly different emotions or feelings between fonts.

I've become somewhat of a type nerd because of my work on the Web. The importance of good typography has become a priority in everything that I do.

I'm not talking about using cool fonts here but rather about *setting* hypertext. For example, Oliver Reichenstein argues in "Web Design is 95% Typography" (http://www.informationarchitects.jp/the-web-is-all-about-typography-period) that

> During the Italian renaissance the typographer had one font to work with, and yet this period produced some of the most beautiful typographical work.

This rings especially true for us Web designers, as we've been plagued by the limited font choices we can depend on being installed by the user.

Oliver goes on to say that

> Information design is not about the use of good typefaces, it is about the use of good typography…. Anyone can use typefaces, some can choose good typefaces, but only few master typography.

So although we're currently limited as to the typefaces we can use on the Web, we can strive to improve the typography while still using those limited typefaces. And by typography I mean the CSS that's currently available to manipulate text with line height, transforming case, letter spacing, size, color, and so forth. A little can go a long way when proper attention is given to typographic principles that have been around ages before the first `<font>` element was typed.

With that in mind, let's talk about a little typographic touch that appears in the Tugboat template and see how it's implemented.

CHANNELING OUR INNER BRINGHURST

It's not exactly light reading material, but I highly recommended Robert Bringhurst's bible on the subject of the art and science of typography, *The Elements of Typographic Style* (**Figure 7.1**).

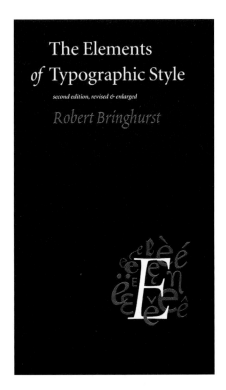

Figure 7.1 Check out *The Elements of Typographic Style*.

The book is filled with guidelines and principles for applying great typography—not specific to the Web, mind you, but to typography in general and its long and storied past. A lot of the book's information can be applied to *hypertext* too, of course, and that's the beauty of typography. It's not about pretty fonts but the manner in which we use them.

Richard Rutter has begun translating Bringhurst's guidelines at http://web-typography.net (**Figure 7.2**), demonstrating how each can be achieved with bulletproof CSS. It's a monster of an undertaking, and here's hoping he continues chipping away at it.

Figure 7.2 Richard Rutter's mammoth undertaking.

GUIDELINE 5.1.3

In Guideline 5.1.3 of *The Elements of Typographic Style*, Bringhurst suggests

> *In heads and titles, use the best available ampersand.*

He explains that frequently the italic version of an ampersand is more decorative and interesting than its roman counterpart, and goes on to explain

> *Since the ampersand is more often used in display work than in ordinary text, the more creative versions are often the more useful. There is rarely any reason not to borrow the italic ampersand for use with roman text.*

I have a soft spot in my heart for the ampersand, so this guideline really stood out, and I immediately thought to apply that thinking to my heads and titles that contain ampersands on the Web. But first a little story.

WE'VE BEEN PROGRESSIVELY ENRICHING SINCE THE VERY BEGINNING

I can remember building my first website. I was living in Allston, Massachusetts, in an apartment that should've probably been condemned. I was earning $5 an hour at a local record label warehouse during the day, and viewing source and hacking away at HTML at night.

I was proud of my first website design. Unfortunately, I've lost the original design and code, but I recall it was an homage to the Atari 2600 (and why not?).

At the time I was obsessed with a futuristic-looking, *free* typeface called Neuropol (**Figure 7.3**). It's unclear why I had such an affinity for this particular font, but it was certainly one that not every viewer of my masterpiece would have installed. I didn't really understand that at the time. I wanted the page to have a cool font in it, and so I chose Neuropol for the title, thinking that's what everyone would see.

This is Neuropol, a free font.

Figure 7.3 I chose this horribly tacky font for my first website.

Lucky for me, whatever program I was using to aid in my HTML authoring at the time created a nice "font stack" for me (and since this was the late '90s, it did so using the now forbidden `<font>` element):

```
<font face="Neuropol, Verdana, Arial, sans-serif">
```

The authoring program was smart enough to include backups in case the user didn't have Neuropol installed. This concept should be well familiar to you, the experienced CSS author—but at the time, without knowing it, my first website was *progressively enriching* the page with a cool font if viewers had it, or a backup if they did not.

I THOUGHT THIS WAS ABOUT AMPERSANDS?

Tying this back to Bringhurst's guidelines, we can apply the simple concept of progressive enrichment regarding available fonts to ampersands that appear in titles and headings on the Web. And we've done just that in the Tugboat template's "Coffee News & Goings On" heading, which Ethan discussed in the previous chapter.

You'll remember Ethan explaining that while the title is set in Georgia, the ampersand is a beautifully ornate italic version set in Baskerville (**Figure 7.4**). Heeding Bringhurst's call, we're using CSS to create a font stack for "the best available" ampersand, with backups for operating systems that might not have Baskerville installed.

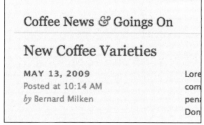

Figure 7.4 On the left, the normal ampersand in Georgia; on the right, the italic version set in Baskerville.

We've wrapped the ampersand in a span element in order to create a reusable class for customizing ampersands in titles throughout the site:

```
<h2>Coffee News <span class="amp">&amp;</span> Goings On</h2>
```

And here again is the CSS declaration that handles the .amp class, where you'll notice a string of fonts listed, each being blessed with a unique, italic version of the ampersand:

```
span.amp {
  font-family: Baskerville, "Goudy Old Style", "Palatino",
➥"Book Antiqua", Georgia, serif;
  font-style: italic;
  }
```

The idea here is that most folks on a Mac will have Baskerville installed, some may be lucky enough to have Goudy Old Style, and even more Windows folks may have Palatino or Book Antiqua. I've ranked these in order of interestingness (**Figure 7.5**), figuring that almost all visitors to the site will get at least a more interesting ampersand than the normal Georgian variety.

Figure 7.5 From left to right, the italic ampersands of Baskerville, Goudy Old Style, Palatino, and Book Antiqua (which you'll notice is based on Palatino).

You could create your own font stacks of course, based on the available ampersands for Mac and Windows—and there are plenty to choose from.

- **Figure 7.6** shows the default fonts installed on the Mac, with some of the more interesting italic ampersands from that pool.

- **Figure 7.7** shows the interesting ampersands from the default fonts installed in Windows XP.

- **Figure 7.8** shows a few of the new typefaces added to Windows Vista, with their interesting ampersands.

Figure 7.6 Mac fonts.

Figure 7.7 Windows XP fonts.

Figure 7.8 Windows Vista fonts.

By glancing over these charts, you could start building your own "Bringhurst ampersand stack," with the most available one to be seen regardless of operating system.

Once again, you have to be okay with the ampersand looking different depending on the situation—but surely by now you've begun to embrace the concept of progressive enrichment, no? And in return, you're left with a simple, flexible way of enhancing typography on the Web, using plain ol' hypertext. A craftsmanship detail indeed.

Font Embedding with CSS

We've been talking about creatively selecting fonts that *some folks* might have installed, but wouldn't it be nice if we as designers had control over what fonts we wished to use and serve them along with the design?

Strides have been made by the pioneering efforts of sIFR (http://wiki.novemberborn.net/sifr3/), a CSS/Flash/JavaScript solution for embedding fonts by replacing hypertext on the page. And more recently, Cufón (http://wiki.github.com/sorccu/cufon/about), which converts fonts to a proprietary format, renders them using JavaScript.

But the future of Web typography just may lie in the hands of @font-face.

Initially introduced back in CSS2, but then later removed in CSS2.1 only to be added back to CSS3, @font-face is an at-rule that allows for embedding font files using CSS declarations.

The best way to explain it is to show it in practice. And oh, is it simple to implement.

ADDING @FONT-FACE TO TUGBOAT

As an example, let's say we wanted to use the beautiful geometric serif, Archer, by Hoefler & Frere-Jones (http://typography.com/fonts/font_overview.php?productLineID=100033) in our Tugboat template, replacing all the Lucida Grande and Georgia that we used previously.

First, we create a declaration that defines the embedded font name and source file using @font-face:

```
@font-face {
  font-family: "Archer Medium";
```

```
  src: url(fonts/Archer-Medium.otf) format("opentype");
}
```

This does two things: 1) it creates an arbitrary name for the font, in this case "Archer Medium" (which can be anything you'd like), and 2) associates that name with a direct link to the font file itself (in this case an OpenType file that lives in a /css/fonts directory).

With that embedded font defined, we can now use the font-family name, Archer Medium, anywhere we'd normally define fonts elsewhere in the CSS — for example, here on the <body> element:

```
body {
  font-family: "Archer Medium", "Lucida Grande", "Lucida
➥Sans Unicode", "Lucida Sans", Helvetica, Arial, sans-serif;
  color: #51463d;
  font-size: 62.5%;
  background: #f3f2e8;
}
```

That's it! **Figure 7.9** shows the Tugboat template set entirely in Archer Medium as viewed in Safari. No scripting, fully resizable/selectable text. There are, um, two little problems, however: A proprietary format to dance around in IE, and a legal can of worms.

Figure 7.9 Our Tugboat template set in Archer Medium (as viewed in Safari).

SUPPORT FOR @FONT-FACE

TIP

For more on @font-face support in browsers, see http://www.webfonts.info/wiki/index.php?title=%40font-face_browser_support.

Is using @font-face a reliable way of handling your Web font needs today? Probably not—but we're getting there and progress is being made. Support for OpenType and TrueType font embedding is present in Safari 3.1+, Firefox 3.5, and Opera 10.

This might come as a shock, but @font-face has also been supported in Internet Explorer since *version 4*—although IE uses a proprietary Microsoft font format called Embedded Open Type (EOT), which no other browser has decided to implement. So while it's possible to get Web fonts working in a large number of browsers, you'll currently need to serve two files: TrueType or OpenType for Safari, Firefox and Opera, and EOT for IE. Check out Jon Tan's article for a method designed to get everyone to play nice using conditional comments: http://jontangerine.com/log/2008/10/font-face-in-ie-making-web-fonts-work.

You could treat this like another opportunity for progressive enrichment and serve OpenType or TrueType Web fonts to everyone but IE and let IE fall back to a default installed font. But we've been harsh enough on Internet Explorer throughout this book, and here's hoping a single format can be decided on for all browsers. Then again, maybe I'm too optimistic.

THE LEGAL STUFF

Possibly more of a problem than the format issue itself is the legal can of worms this direct linking of font files opens up. Much like the music industry scurrying to adjust to the digital age, typographers and font foundries are terrified at the prospect that their font files would be directly accessible via a URL and susceptible to piracy. Currently very few foundries offer a @font-face-specific license for their fonts, and some even prohibit it.

For example, the wonderful Archer typeface that we used earlier would be a no-go as a Web font, as the foundry, Hoefler & Frere-Jones, clearly states that use of @font-face is prohibited under their end-user license agreement.

What's needed is a legal way of linking to font files that benefits the foundries while still letting the CSS designer maintain control. I have faith that something will be worked out soon, as surely embedded fonts on the Web is the way forward.

USING FREE FONTS, FOR NOW

Legal woes aside, that doesn't mean you can't start experimenting and using `@font-face` today. It just means you should be very careful about the fonts you choose to embed. Thankfully, many perfectly usable *free* fonts are available that you can plug in and use *right now* in the browsers that support Web fonts.

Take, for example, Jos Buivenga's free font foundry, exljbris shown in **Figure 7.10** (bonus points if you can tell me how to pronounce that). Jos has been creating high-quality free fonts, while also allowing font embedding (with attribution) as part of the font's license.

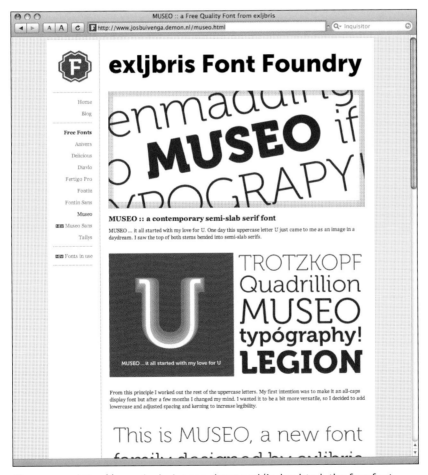

Figure 7.10 http://www.josbuivenga.demon.nl/index.html, the free font foundry of Jos Buivenga.

Figure 7.11 shows the Tugboat template set completely in Museo Medium using @font-face, one of Buivenga's wonderful free fonts. This is a nice example of something we can use today. Right now. And it only scratches the surface of what's possible (and what will eventually be possible) when more typographic variety is added to the Web designer's toolbox.

Figure 7.11 Our Tugboat template set completely in Museo Medium using @font-face.

So, the story of embedded Web fonts is far from over—but it's exciting that things are starting to gather steam. With Firefox 3.5 adding support for @font-face rules, we might be reaching the tipping point in terms of actual real-world use. If the legal issues can be worked out between the foundries and Web designers, and if IE adds support for TrueType and OpenType formats, then typography on the Web will surely never be the same.

Like with the other CSS3 goodies we've discussed in this book, the time to start experimenting is *now*. You'll get a leg up on the technologies that will be commonplace in the future, and in certain circumstances you'll be able to utilize these new tools today.

TYPEKIT

The folks at Small Batch Inc. have announced an exciting development that just may make Web fonts a reality for designers. Here's the scoop on Typekit (http://typekit.com), in their own words:

> We've been working with foundries to develop a consistent Web-only font linking license. We've built a technology platform that lets us host both free and commercial fonts in a way that is incredibly fast, smoothes out differences in how browsers handle type, and offers the level of protection that type designers need without resorting to annoying and ineffective DRM.
>
> As a Typekit user, you'll have access to our library of high-quality fonts. Just add a line of JavaScript to your markup, tell us what fonts you want to use, and then craft your pages the way you always have. Except now you'll be able to use real fonts. This really is going to change Web design.

Hats off to Small Batch for doing something about the legal woes with font embedding rather than just complaining that there's no viable solution. We'll be keeping a close eye on this product as a legal way of handling embedded Web fonts going forward. And what's most exciting is that Typekit's existence will only help push all of this stuff forward in a positive direction. Progress.

jQuery

Switching gears away from typography, let's next talk briefly about JavaScript. I've never written about JavaScript before, and I consider myself a dabbler in such behavior. But being a designer who lives and breathes CSS, jQuery (**Figure 7.12** on the next page) struck a chord, because it allows me to quickly and easily add behavioral effects to my interfaces in a familiar way.

jQuery is a self-described

> ... fast and concise JavaScript Library that simplifies HTML document traversing, event handling, animating, and Ajax interactions for rapid Web development. jQuery is designed to change the way that you write JavaScript.

Figure 7.12 The jQuery JavaScript library, found at http://jquery.com.

In other words, a JavaScript library will make it easier for you to write often-used design patterns for your interfaces. There are many libraries out there, but I instantly took a liking to jQuery's CSS-like selector syntax for attaching events, effects, and so forth to specific elements. It just clicked.

The core of jQuery is contained in a single .js file—but there's also a large community contributing plug-ins for everything imaginable that can be done with JavaScript.

HOW I USE JQUERY IN TUGBOAT

There are two places I use jQuery to handle some subtle details in the Tugboat template, and while they only scratch the surface of the power of jQuery, I thought it'd be helpful to point out how simple and flexible it is to add effects and handle common UI patterns for those of us whose strength lies more on the CSS side of things.

Slide out "Advanced Options"

If we look at the "Find a Location" search bar in the Tugboat template (**Figure 7.13**), you'll notice a little link in the bottom right that offers "Advanced Options." This is a common pattern in many interfaces, where you want a link to dynamically expose a hidden chunk of content, additional form fields, and similar uses. Clicking the link again will hide the chunk.

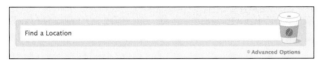

Figure 7.13 Notice the Advanced Options link.

In the case of Tugboat, clicking the link exposes a (very old) map that instructs you to indicate your location (**Figure 7.14**).

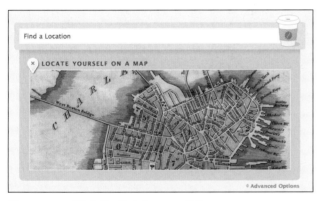

Figure 7.14 Click the link to open this map.

JavaScript is a perfect facilitator here, enabling the map (which could be permanently in the markup regardless of whether it's visible on the page) to magically appear and disappear with the click of a link—all without the page refreshing. I'm sure you've had to tackle this little hide/show widget type situation before.

Historically I'd Google for a script that would hide and show an element, and I'd customize it to my particular markup and style. I'd probably do this each time I needed to accomplish this kind of trickery, and I might not have used the same exact script each time. In other words, I was a scripting *hack*.

Now jQuery has this sort of thing baked right into it (among many other benefits). And not only does jQuery make it simple to hide and show elements of your choosing, but it makes it incredibly easy to add effects to those actions as well. Let's take a look.

Linking the jQuery source

After downloading the latest version of jQuery (which is just a single .js file), just reference it in the <head> of the document like so:

```
<head>
  . . .
  <script src="js/jquery-1.3.2.min.js" type="text/
➥javascript"></script>
</head>
```

In the case of Tugboat, we're using the most current, compressed version of the jQuery source (.min.js) for speed.

With the script in place, you're now ready to take advantage of all the goodies that come along with jQuery. Next we'll build a little function to handle the Advanced Options toggle.

Marking up the map

In terms of marking up the form, we want to include all the content that will be shown after the link is clicked. That means we'll code the map as we'd like it to appear and hide it later with CSS.

```
<form class="group" action="/">
  <fieldset>
    <img src="img/cup.png" alt="coffee cup" />
    <input name-"location" type="text" value="Find a
➥Location" />
  </fieldset>

  <fieldset>
    <label>Locate Yourself on a Map</label>
    <img src="img/map.jpg" alt="map" />
    <img src="img/place-marker.png" alt="marker" />
  </fieldset>

  <div>
    <a href="#map">Advanced Options</a>
  </div>
</form>
```

NOTE

Since Tugboat is a fictional site, the map is simply a static and nonfunctional image. Perhaps someday, when the curly braces and angle brackets get old, I'll open up shop for real, brewing beans and marking foam. Until then...

With the basic form markup in place, let's add some `id`s for styling purposes:

```
<form id="loc" class="group" action="/">
  <fieldset id="location">
  <img id="cup" src="img/cup.png" alt="coffee cup" />
  <input id="loc-text" name="location" type="text"
⮑value="Find a Location" />
  </fieldset>

  <fieldset id="map">
    <label>Locate Yourself on a Map</label>
    <img src="img/map.jpg" alt="map" id="map-img" />
    <img src="img/place-marker.png" alt="marker"
⮑id="marker" />
  </fieldset>

  <div id="loc-adv">
    <a href="#map">Advanced Options</a>
  </div>
</form>
```

Identifying the pieces

These semantic `id`s will be useful for positioning and styling the various elements of the form, but most important, attaching the `#map` id will allow us to hide the map completely with CSS using `display: none;`:

```
#map {
  display: none;
  margin: 0 1em;
  padding: 2em;
  background: #d5d4c7 url(../img/map-shadow.gif) repeat-x
⮑top left;
  }
```

So while the styles are in place to make the map look and behave the way we'd like it to, at first load it'll also be hidden from view due to that initial `display: none;` rule.

Remember how the `href` to "Advanced Options" is really just a jump to the `#map` id?

```
  <div id="loc-adv">
    <a href="#map">Advanced Options</a>
  </div>
```

This will ensure the link makes sense in a device that doesn't support CSS (or JavaScript)—the link doesn't go to a different URL; instead, it's an anchor to where the map is on the page. We'll let jQuery intercept that action, and attach the show/hide functionality to the click.

Creating the jQuery function

Now that we have the map hidden, the link in place, and `id`s on the elements we need them on, we can write the simple little jQuery function that will attach the hide/show event to the right pieces on the page.

As I mentioned earlier, one of the reasons I love using jQuery is that its selector syntax is familiar to those who work with CSS. Traversing elements and attaching events is as easy as writing a selector for a style sheet.

For instance, the following is the little script that toggles the *#map* off and on. The `toggle()`; is a built-in jQuery function that will hide a chosen element if it's visible, and show it if it's hidden. By attaching that effect to the click of a specific link (in our case, the `<a>` inside the `<div id="loc-adv">`), we get the hide/show functionality we're looking for when we click Advanced Options:

NOTE

I've added the function to the *<head>* of the document (after linking the jQuery core file), but you could keep your functions in an external file as well.

```
<head>
  <script src="js/jquery-1.2.6.min.js"
➥type="text/javascript"></script>
  <script type="text/javascript">
    // Toggle advanced options
    $(document).ready(function(){
      $("#loc-adv a").click(function(){
        $("#map").toggle();
        return false;
      });
    });
  </script>
</head>
```

With that little snippet of JavaScript, a user can hide/show the map at will by clicking Advanced Options. You can see that attaching this sort of functionality is almost as simple as writing CSS declarations—and the markup is free and clear of any inline JavaScript. jQuery does all the heavy lifting for you, and traverses the DOM to find the right elements and execute the function on them.

Making things more interesting with slideToggle();

Another great thing about jQuery is that not only does it handle your DOM selection needs in a familiar way, it also puts a big bag of tricks at your disposal.

As an elementary example, instead of using `toggle();` to hide and show the map in Tugboat, we could swap that out with `slideToggle();`, which will add a slide effect to the hide/show event. Clicking Advanced Options will now reveal the map by sliding it down underneath the Find a Location field (**Figure 7.15**). It's a fantastic effect, and it's all achieved by swapping one little line of code in our function, thanks to jQuery's built-in effects:

```
<head>
  <script src="js/jquery-1.2.6.min.js"
➥type="text/javascript"></script>
  <script type="text/javascript">
    // Toggle advanced options
    $(document).ready(function(){
      $("#loc-adv a").click(function(){
        $("#map").slideToggle("slow");
        return false;
      });
    });
  </script>
</head>
```

Figure 7.15 Once again, I find myself wishing I could embed video into these pages. Imagine the map sliding down from the location bar. It's far more exciting in person.

You'll notice the `slow` parameter added to the `slideToggle();` function. `slow` is one of three values allowed for adjusting the speed of the sliding animation (the other values are `normal` and `fast`).

Far more effects are available to the jQuery developer—among them toggling, sliding, fading, and creating custom animation. All are available with a simple syntax that taps into the jQuery core file that you're importing into the document.

USING JQUERY TO ADD A .LAST CLASS

I'm using jQuery again in the Tugboat template, this time to auto-add a .last class in certain lists on the page.

What do I mean by a .last class? You're probably familiar with this scenario: You have a list of items, each styled with margins and padding and perhaps a bottom border to separate each line. But for the last item in the list, you'd like it to have slightly different styles—less bottom margin and/or no border, for instance. Often I'll add a <li class="last"> to that last item in order to override default styles for that particular item. If the list changes or grows, it requires me to be diligent about moving that .last to the very last list item each time.

Adding a .last to the Press list on Tugboat

At the right sidebar in the Tugboat template there's a "Press" section, which is a list of thrilling and important quotes from the media (**Figure 7.16**).

Figure 7.16 The Press section.

The markup for this little section consists of an unordered list, each containing a <blockquote> with a quote and attribution:

```
<ul class="press">
  <li>
    <blockquote>
      <p>&#8220;Tugboat Coffee just may be the most amazing
➥coffee I've ever tasted.&#8221;</p>
      <p class="author">&#8212; Martin Farmer,
➥<cite>BeanzMag</cite></p>
    </blockquote>
  </li>
  <li>
    <blockquote>
      <p>&#8220;A rare treasure, amongst coffee-related web
➥sites. If six stars were possible, I&#8217;d rate it
➥&#8230; seven.&#8221;</p>
      <p class="author">&#8212; <cite>Bean There, Drunk
➥That</cite></p>
    </blockquote>
  </li>
  <li>
    <blockquote>
      <p>&#8220;Mmmmm...&#8221;</p>
      <p class="author">&#8212; <cite>Happy Customer
➥</cite></p>
    </blockquote>
  </li>
</ul>
```

The styling for each quote is relatively minimal. Each list item is separated by some margins, padding, and a 1-pixel horizontal rule at the bottom.

Block quotes and author attribution get their own styles as well, mostly text treatment and spacing adjustments:

```
ul.press li {
  margin: 1em 0;
  padding: 0 0 1em 0;
  border-bottom: 1px solid #e2e1d4;
  }
ul.press li blockquote {
  font-family: Georgia, serif;
  font-size: 1.2em;
  font-style: italic;                      (continued on next page)
```

```
line-height: 1.5em;
    }
ul.press li blockquote p {
  margin: 0 0 1em 0;
    }
ul.press li blockquote p.author {
  margin: 0;
  font-family: "Lucida Grande", "Lucida Sans Unicode",
➥"Lucida Sans", Helvetica, Arial, sans-serif;
  font-size: .8em;
  text-align: right;
  color: #9c836e;
    }
ul.press li blockquote p.author a {
  font-weight: bold;
    }
```

As **Figure 7.17** shows, each list item now gets a bottom border, including the last item in the list. But we actually want the border (and padding) to be absent on the last item.

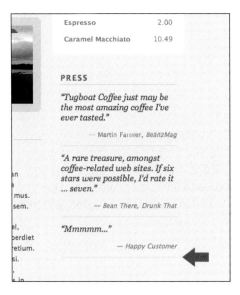

Figure 7.17 Each list item has a bottom border, even the last item.

To override the default styling of having a `border-bottom` and `padding-bottom`, we can add a `.last` class to the last item in the list:

```
<ul class="press">
...
  <li class="last">
    <blockquote>
      <p>&#8220;Mmmmm...&#8221;</p>
      <p class="author">&#8212; <cite>Happy Customer
➥</cite></p>
    </blockquote>
  </li>
</ul>
```

And then write a quick declaration that turns off the border and padding for that class:

```
ul.press li.last {
  padding-bottom: 0;
  border-bottom: none;
  }
```

That'll meet our needs just fine—but in many situations, it's an annoyance to have to remember to move that class to the last item should the list be edited, added to, chopped down, or otherwise modified. In addition, should the list be automatically generated by a backend content management system (CMS) or development framework, you'll need to ensure the logic is in there to attach this class to the last item.

In other words, in some situations it might not be a big deal to add the class manually. And in other situations it can become a nuisance, or something that could be overlooked eventually.

If you're already using jQuery to handle your scripting needs, then we can skip adding the class to the markup altogether. We'll let jQuery's DOM traversing handle that automatically; it will find the last item in the list dynamically as the page loads, then add that class to the appropriate item. jQuery assumes the burden of maintaining where that last class is inserted, whether it be manually or programmatically (by a backend system).

We'll keep the CSS declaration as is. A class of .last on a list item turns off the border and padding:

```
ul.press li.last {
  padding-bottom: 0;
  border-bottom: none;
  }
```

But instead of adding the class in the markup, we'll write up a little jQuery function to do that for us (we'll add it to the previous jQuery example in the <head>):

```
<head>
  <script src="js/jquery-1.2.6.min.js"
➥type="text/javascript"></script>
  <script type="text/javascript">
    // Toggle advanced options
    $(document).ready(function(){
      $("#loc-adv a").click(function(){
        $("#map").slideToggle("slow");
        return false;
      });
    });

    // Add .last class to certain lists
    $(document).ready(function(){
      $("ul.press li:last").addClass("last");
    });
  </script>
</head>
```

Using one of jQuery's filter selectors (:last), we're essentially saying here, "Find the last <li> element within <ul class="press"> and add the .last class to it."

Done.

Presentation or behavior?

For more thoughts on how JavaScript could further patch our CSS needs, check out Eric Meyer's article "JavaScript Will Save Us All": http://meyerweb .com/eric/thoughts/2008/10/22/ javascript-will-save-us-all/.

In a sense, we're using JavaScript to fill in the holes that would likely be better solved with CSS. Where JavaScript is best served controlling *behavior* on the page, we're using it here for purely a *presentational* reason. That's normally not a smart route to take—but in this case (if you're already leveraging jQuery for other tasks) it's a tiny function, and one that would degrade just fine should JavaScript be off or unsupported (there'd simply be a border on the bottom with some extra padding).

What about :last-child?

Also included in CSS3 is the `:last-child` pseudo-class, which would essentially solve the problem even more effectively. We still wouldn't need to add a class in the markup, but rather just alter the declaration that turns off the border and padding using this pseudo-class:

```
ul.press li:last-child {
  padding-bottom: 0;
  border-bottom: none;
  }
```

Now *this* is certainly ideal, but unfortunately it isn't supported in Internet Explorer (or Safari 3.0 and below). If the appearance of the border in those browsers is okay with you, though, by all means progressively enrich here.

TIP

For the curious, the inverse `:first-child` pseudo-class was a part of CSS2 and is unsupported in IE6, and is somewhat problematic in IE7 and IE8. See http://www.quirksmode.org/css/contents.html for more compatibility comparisons.

SCRATCHING THE SURFACE

While I've just shared two, tiny ways I've used the jQuery framework in the Tugboat template, I've only just scratched the surface in terms of what it can do. Aside from its single core file, jQuery also has a vibrant community of JavaScript developers, who have extended the framework to accomplish a variety of useful tasks via plug-ins.

Regardless of which JavaScript framework you use (or if you roll your own scripting code yourself), the takeaway here is that JavaScript can be an important player in crafting those interface details that elevate a great user experience. Personally, I've found jQuery to be a familiar, exciting way to elegantly add behavior and interactions to my designs.

Shifting Backgrounds (Parallax Scrolling for the Lazy)

And finally, here's an almost invisible touch (*tips cap to Phil Collins*) that acts as a nice summation of what a craftsmanship detail really is.

Unseen by some who might miss it, but sure to put a smile on the face who do notice it, the "parallax scrolling background" effect is a simple way of embracing the fluidity of the Web as its own medium, but taking some extra time to add *movement* to something seemingly static.

GUERRILLA (OR GORILLA?) TACTICS

I first became aware of the "parallax scrolling" effect after seeing Clearleft's site for Silverback (see **Figure 7.18**), a nifty piece of software that allows you to conduct on-the-spot usability testing.

And while the software *is* excellent, it was the execution of the site's design that I specifically took note of. In particular, I was impressed by the way the vines hanging down over the gorilla seem to take on a three-dimensional appearance when the browser window's width is resized. Squeezing the window's width in and out makes the three layers of vines slide horizontally—at different speeds. The frontmost layer blurs to create even more depth. The result is remarkable, and I wasted probably an hour sliding the window back and forth while quietly chuckling.

It was probably less than an hour.

Figure 7.18 Silverback usability software by Clearleft: http://silverbackapp.com. Try resizing your browser window, and watch the jungle vines shift at different speeds.

The term "parallax" comes from arcade games of the 1980s, where background images move slower across the screen than those in the foreground. It mimics a 3D environment in a flat, 2D game. See http://en.wikipedia.org/wiki/Parallax_scrolling.

Seemingly invisible details

This dimensional effect via browser window resizing illustrates the epitome of a craftsmanship detail—one that takes effort and care to implement, but also one that might not even be seen by every visitor. We've spent a good portion of this book talking about details that may differ depending on the browser being used, and the importance of letting go of the control that seeks to homogenize the visual design.

The parallax effect embraces the fact that window widths are moving targets. They're impossible to count on and will always be a variable. Instead of locking down graphics to specific positions on the page, why not split them up and let them interact with one another? The fluid grids that Ethan discussed in the previous chapter are an even more extreme example of this acceptance.

How it's done

Paul Annett describes how he achieved the parallax effect on the Silverback site in his article "How to recreate Silverback's parallax effect" (http://thinkvitamin.com/features/how-to-recreate-silverbacks-parallax-effect/). And it involves the layering of three horizontally repeating PNG images, each set with a horizontal position using differing percentages.

Here, I'll generalize the code greatly, but by assigning three stacked layers of background images at 20%, 40%, and 150%, you'll get each horizontally tiling layer moving along with the browser window's width at different speeds:

```
body {
  background: url(../img/vines-back.png) repeat-x 20% 0;
  }
#container {
  background: url(../img/vines-middle.png) repeat-x 40% 0;
  }
#container-inner {
  background: url(../img/vines-front.png) repeat-x 150% 0;
  }
```

It's a clever trick, and one that has endless possibilities in terms of what you can layer, how many layers you can use, and the speed differential among them all.

Experimenting with negative percentages

Toward the end of Paul's article, he mentions the interesting results of using *negative* percentages to horizontally position the background images (tipping his hat to *The Rissington Podcast* (http://therissingtonpodcast.co.uk) site, also mentioned back in Chapter 5, which also boasts a parallax scrolling effect in its design).

Using a negative percentage to position backgrounds makes the images appear to be moving to the left, often in the reverse direction that the window is resizing (if you're grabbing the lower-right corner of the browser window and pulling right, the images move in the opposite direction). And, as Paul notes in the article, the higher the negative percentage, the faster it will move.

PARALLAX EFFECT FOR THE LAZY

Taking Paul Annett's tutorial and simplifying things a bit, I started applying the negative percentage horizontal placement any time I was dealing with horizontally tiling background images. Even if it's a single image tiling over a background color, having the image move in the opposite direction as the resized browser window yields an effect similar to that of the multilayered parallax method—with far less work.

How it's done on Tugboat

For example, on the Tugboat template, there is a background image that creates the sky, clouds, and rolling hills of coffee in the page header (**Figure 7.19**). This 1024- by 56-pixel image is tiled horizontally so that no matter how wide the visitor's browser window is, the header will always extend seamlessly from side to side.

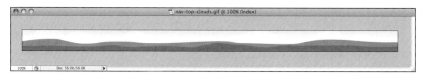

Figure 7.19 Our background image that will tile horizontally.

The image is layered on top of a header that's the same color brown as the bottom of the hills so that it can sit at the top, while the header can extend to any height it needs to.

In addition, a horizontally tiled gradient image sits at the *bottom* of the header (**Figure 7.20**). The gradient fades from a darker brown, up into the lighter brown header color.

Figure 7.20 The gradient fades from dark brown to the lighter brown header color.

We'll need two containing elements around the header's content in order to layer these background images in the right spots (clouds and hills on top, gradient along the bottom, as shown in **Figure 7.21**).

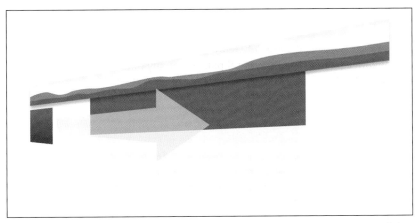

Figure 7.21 We have a 3D view of the clouds/hills image tiling on top and the gradient image tiling along the bottom of the brown header.

Tugboat's header markup

Here's the markup we'll use to structure Tugboat's header, which includes the logo, tagline, tugboat graphic, and navigation list.

```
<div id="header" class="group"><div id="header-inner">
  <div id="nav" class="group">
    <div id="logo" class="group">
      <h1><img src="img/logo-lofi.gif" alt="Tugboat" /></h1>
      <p>Pulling you along since 2009.</p>
    </div>

    <img src="img/tugboat.png" alt="tugboat" id="tugboat" />

    <ul class="group">
      <li><a href="#"><strong>Home <em>News and Trends</em>
➥</strong></a></li>
      <li><a href="#"><strong>Our Coffee <em>Handcrafted
➥Beans</em></strong></a></li>
      <li><a href="#"><strong>Store <em>Shop Online</em>
➥</strong></a></li>
```

(continued on next page)

```
        <li><a href="#"><strong>About <em>Company Info</em>
➥</strong></a></li>
      </ul>
    </div>
  </div>
</div></div> <!-- /header -->
```

Note the *two* outer container `<div>`s labeled `#header` and `#header-inner`. These are the two elements that we'll use to layer the background images on while also specifying the brown background color.

Adding the background images

First, we'll layer the gradient image that runs along the bottom of the header, over the brown background. There's also a single-pixel white border on the bottom to create a little detail separation between the header and tan page background:

```
#header {
  border-bottom: 1px solid #fff;
  background: #766557 url(../img/h-bg-bottom.gif)
➥repeat-x bottom left;
  }
```

Next, we'll layer the horizontally repeating clouds and hills image that runs along the top of the header by attaching it as a background image to `#header-inner`:

```
#header {
  border-bottom: 1px solid #fff;
  background: #766557 url(../img/h-bg-bottom.gif)
➥repeat x bottom left;
  }
#header-inner {
  padding: 70px 0 0;
  background: url(../img/nav-top-clouds.gif)
➥repeat-x top left;
  }
```

Figure 7.22 shows the results of those tiling images. This approach ensures that no matter how wide the browser window is, the clouds/hills and gradient will meet the edges of the window seamlessly.

Figure 7.22 The result of our tiling images.

Negative percentages for horizontally tiling images

Now to get back to the lazy parallax method, all we need to change is the horizontal positioning of the clouds/hills image using a high *negative* percentage (remember, the higher the percentage, the faster speed the image will appear to move):

```
#header-inner {
  padding: 70px 0 0 0;
  background: url(../img/nav-top-clouds.gif) repeat-x -80% 0;
  }
```

Here we've changed the background position to -80% horizontally, and 0 (or top) vertically. That's it.

Now when visitors adjust their browser's width, they'll see the clouds and hills shift in the background in the opposite direction of the window. It's a parallax-esque effect for one-third the price!

A characteristic of craftsmanship

Again, not everyone is going to notice this subtle detail, but it's incredibly *simple* to implement. Try experimenting with negative percentages any time you have a horizontally repeating background image. I, for one, will be pleasantly surprised when I see it.

Conclusion

Well, my friends, we've come to the end of the book. As I type this the days are getting longer, the birds are chirping, and the trees are blossoming. There's something new in the spring air (aside from sneeze-inducing pollen).

To me, it feels like a lot of exciting things are happening in the world of Web design. I hope that by navigating through these pages, you'll be inspired to start experimenting with some of this new, exciting stuff—keeping in mind the bulletproof principles that help craft good Web designs into great ones.

I hope you've enjoyed hearing Ethan and I talk about what impresses us when implementing design on the Web: that details do matter, and prioritizing those details matters even more. So much of Web design is convincing yourself you're doing the right thing. And I hope we've played a small part in assisting in those decisions.

As for the Tugboat Coffee Company, like I mentioned, when I begin to tire of angle brackets and curly braces, perhaps I'll open up shop for real. First cup is on me.

Cheers.

Index

Index

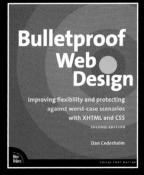